P9-CKJ-751

Readings on The scarlet
letter /
c1998.
33305010061616
MH   05/21/98

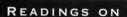

READINGS ON

THE
SCARLET
LETTER

SANTA CLARA COUNTY LIBRARY

3 3305 01006 1616

OTHER TITLES IN THE GREENHAVEN PRESS LITERARY COMPANION SERIES:

AMERICAN AUTHORS

Maya Angelou
Stephen Crane
Emily Dickinson
William Faulkner
F. Scott Fitzgerald
Nathaniel Hawthorne
Ernest Hemingway
Herman Melville
Arthur Miller
Eugene O'Neill
Edgar Allan Poe
John Steinbeck
Mark Twain

BRITISH AUTHORS

Jane Austen
Joseph Conrad
Charles Dickens

WORLD AUTHORS

Fyodor Dostoyevsky
Homer
Sophocles

AMERICAN LITERATURE

The Great Gatsby
Of Mice and Men

BRITISH LITERATURE

Animal Farm
The Canterbury Tales
Lord of the Flies
Romeo and Juliet
Shakespeare: The Comedies
Shakespeare: The Sonnets
Shakespeare: The Tragedies
A Tale of Two Cities

WORLD LITERATURE

Diary of a Young Girl

THE GREENHAVEN PRESS
Literary Companion
TO AMERICAN LITERATURE

READINGS ON

THE SCARLET LETTER

David Bender, *Publisher*

Bruno Leone, *Executive Editor*

Scott Barbour, *Senior Editor*

Bonnie Szumski, *Series Editor*

Eileen Morey, *Book Editor*

Greenhaven Press, San Diego, CA

Every effort has been made to trace the owners of copy-righted material. The articles in this volume may have been edited for content, length, and/or reading level. The titles have been changed to enhance the editorial purpose of the Opposing Viewpoints® concept. Those interested in locating the original source will find the complete citation on the first page of each article.

Library of Congress Cataloging-in-Publication Data

Readings on The scarlet letter / Eileen Morey, book editor.
    p.   cm. — (The Greenhaven Press literary
companion to American literature)
    Includes bibliographical references and index.
    ISBN 1-56510-757-8 (lib. bdg. : alk. paper). —
ISBN 1-56510-756-X (pbk. : alk. paper)
    1. Hawthorne, Nathaniel, 1804–1864. Scarlet letter.
2. Historical fiction, American—History and criticism.
3. Mothers and daughters in literature. 4. Massachusetts
—In literature. 5. Puritans in literature. 6. Adultery in
literature. 7. Women in literature. I. Morey, Eileen,
1923–   . II. Series.
PS1868.R39   1998
813'.3—dc21   97-22684
                                                          CIP

Cover photo: North Wind Picture Archives

No part of this book may be reproduced or used in any form or by any means, electrical, mechanical, or otherwise, including, but not limited to, photocopy, recording, or any information storage and retrieval system, without prior written permission from the publisher.

Copyright ©1998 by Greenhaven Press, Inc.
PO Box 289009
San Diego, CA 92198-9009
Printed in the U.S.A.

"On the breast of her gown, in red cloth, surrounded with an elaborate embroidery and fantastic flourishes of gold thread, appeared the letter A."

—*The Scarlet Letter*

CONTENTS

The characters of Hester, Dimmesdale, Pearl, and Chillingworth are some of the most complex and symbolic in all of American literature.

Chapter 3: Major Themes

FOREWORD

"'Tis the good reader that
makes the good book."

Ralph Waldo Emerson

The story's bare facts are simple: The captain, an old and scarred seafarer, walks with a peg leg made of whale ivory. He relentlessly drives his crew to hunt the world's oceans for the great white whale that crippled him. After a long search, the ship encounters the whale and a fierce battle ensues. Finally the captain drives his harpoon into the whale, but the harpoon line catches the captain about the neck and drags him to his death.

A simple story, a straightforward plot—yet, since the 1851 publication of Herman Melville's *Moby-Dick*, readers and critics have found many meanings in the struggle between Captain Ahab and the whale. To some, the novel is a cautionary tale that depicts how Ahab's obsession with revenge leads to his insanity and death. Others believe that the whale represents the unknowable secrets of the universe and that Ahab is a tragic hero who dares to challenge fate by attempting to discover this knowledge. Perhaps Melville intended Ahab as a criticism of Americans' tendency to become involved in well-intentioned but irrational causes. Or did Melville model Ahab after himself, letting his fictional character express his anger at what he perceived as a cruel and distant god?

Although literary critics disagree over the meaning of *Moby-Dick*, readers do not need to choose one particular interpretation in order to gain an understanding of Melville's novel. Instead, by examining various analyses, they can gain numerous insights into the issues that lie under the surface of the basic plot. Studying the writings of literary critics can also aid readers in making their own assessments of *Moby-Dick* and other literary works and in developing analytical thinking skills.

The Greenhaven Literary Companion Series was created with these goals in mind. Designed for young adults, this unique anthology series provides an engaging and comprehensive introduction to literary analysis and criticism. The essays included in the Literary Companion Series are chosen for their accessibility to a young adult audience and are expertly edited in consideration of both the reading and comprehension levels of this audience. In addition, each essay is introduced by a concise summation that presents the contributing writer's main themes and insights. Every anthology in the Literary Companion Series contains a varied selection of critical essays that cover a wide time span and express diverse views. Wherever possible, primary sources are represented through excerpts from authors' notebooks, letters, and journals and through contemporary criticism.

Each title in the Literary Companion Series pays careful consideration to the historical context of the particular author or literary work. In-depth biographies and detailed chronologies reveal important aspects of authors' lives and emphasize the historical events and social milieu that influenced their writings. To facilitate further research, every anthology includes primary and secondary source bibliographies of articles and/or books selected for their suitability for young adults. These engaging features make the Greenhaven Literary Companion Series ideal for introducing students to literary analysis in the classroom or as a library resource for young adults researching the world's great authors and literature.

Exceptional in its focus on young adults, the Greenhaven Literary Companion Series strives to present literary criticism in a compelling and accessible format. Every title in the series is intended to spark readers' interest in leading American and world authors, to help them broaden their understanding of literature, and to encourage them to formulate their own analyses of the literary works that they read. It is the editors' hope that young adult readers will find these anthologies to be true companions in their study of literature.

INTRODUCTION

The Scarlet Letter remains a prominent contribution to American literature. Hester Prynne remains one of the most well-known of heroines. Proving its merit for generations of readers, *The Scarlet Letter* continues to head lists of great American books and required high school reading lists.

It is fitting that America's first great novel should be set in one of its first settlements. Yet the main conflict of the book—the effect of guilt on those who have committed an act determined by society to be evil—is as relevant today as it was in 1850. Hawthorne's artful mixture of symbols and allegory, well-developed characters, accurate portrayal of attitudes and behaviors, and sustained mood makes *The Scarlet Letter* a memorable book. However, those readers who expect to find a happy ending with all the knots securely tied will be disappointed. Most critics agree that Hawthorne rules out atonement for his wayward lead characters.

The Greenhaven Literary Companion to Nathaniel Hawthorne's *The Scarlet Letter* includes critical essays selected to give teachers and students both broad and detailed understanding of the book. The authors consider particular points of interest—symbolism, for example—in detail, but not always in agreement.

Some critics have called Hawthorne's work outdated, but some highly regarded writers—Herman Melville, Henry James, William Faulkner—have acknowledged a debt to Nathaniel Hawthorne. The themes of his books and tales—hidden guilt, mind ruling the heart, the effects of wrongdoing on subsequent generations—are still relevant. Literary critic and Hawthorne biographer Mark Van Doren points out that man's conscience is as accountable today as it was a century and a half ago and will be a century and a half hence. *The Scarlet Letter* was, is, and will remain a literary masterpiece.

NATHANIEL HAWTHORNE: HAUNTED BY THE GUILT OF HIS ANCESTORS

Most people considered Nathaniel Hawthorne a fortunate man. First, he maintained a happy marriage with his wife, Sophia, and both of them were delighted with their three children, despite financial struggles through several lean years. Second, he was a popular writer in his own time. Third, the writers and poets Hawthorne associated with and drew sustenance from were a virtual roster of American literary greats: Ralph Waldo Emerson, Herman Melville, Henry David Thoreau, Bronson Alcott, William Ellery Channing, Oliver Wendell Holmes, Henry Wadsworth Longfellow, John Greenleaf Whittier, and James Russell Lowell.

HAWTHORNE ASSUMES THE GUILT OF HIS ANCESTORS

Yet, in these enviable circumstances Hawthorne remained essentially as he describes himself in the preface to the 1851 edition of *Twice-Told Tales:* "mild, shy, gentle, melancholic." Why? What was shading his life? Literary scholars over the years have settled on one probable cause of Hawthorne's innate despair: He was burdened by the misdeeds of his notorious Puritan ancestors. Scholars have concluded, and Hawthorne himself agreed with his contemporary critics, that he had assumed the guilt of his Puritan grandfathers.

His great-great-great-grandfather William Hathorne migrated to America with the Puritans in 1630. In "The Custom-House," the autobiographical introduction to *The Scarlet Letter*, Nathaniel describes this ancestor as "a soldier, legislator, judge; he was a ruler in the church; he had all the Puritan traits, both good and evil." History records that William Hathorne once ordered that a burglar be branded with a *B* on his forehead; another time he sentenced a Quaker woman to be whipped through the streets of Salem and then driven into the wilderness. His son John, Nathaniel's great-great-grandfather, was a prosecuting—and a persecuting—magistrate at the infamous 1692 witch trials in Salem, Massachusetts. Nathaniel adds in "The Custom-House," "I, the present writer, as their representative, hereby take shame upon myself for their sakes." Despite this affiliation, however, Hawthorne added a *w* to his name when he began to write for publication, perhaps to distance himself from his ancestors.

The next three generations of Hathornes were not so prominent. John's son Joseph was a farmer in Salem township. His son Daniel became a sea captain, as did Daniel's son Nathaniel, father of the author. When Nathaniel Sr. married Elizabeth Manning, they moved in with his widowed mother and his two sisters in Salem. The couple had three children: Elizabeth, born in 1802; Nathaniel Jr., on July 4, 1804; and Louisa, in 1808. Nathaniel Jr. was only four years old when his father died of fever in Dutch Guiana. Never having seen much of his seafaring father, the young Nathaniel hardly missed him. They had been poor before; now, with no income, they turned to Elizabeth's family. The Mannings, who were hospitable people, accepted Elizabeth and her brood into their already crowded home.

HAWTHORNE'S CHILDHOOD

Nathaniel's four aunts and four uncles were kind to the children, especially to Nathaniel, who was for a few early years frail and often ill. He gradually grew stronger, but at the age of nine, during a ball game at school, Nathaniel injured his foot. Housebound, he eventually could walk with crutches, but it took two years for him to fully regain the use of his foot. During the months of confinement, the schoolmaster came to the house every morning to hear his lessons, and Nathaniel freely indulged his love of reading. Spenser's *Faerie Queene* and Bunyon's *Pilgrim's Progress*, as well as Shakespeare's plays, were among his favorites. The long hours he spent alone established in him a lifelong habit of solitude.

In 1816, when Hawthorne's foot was completely recovered and he was otherwise in good health, Elizabeth and the children went to live in Raymond, Maine, where the Manning family owned a house and some property. Young Hawthorne reveled in the freedom of the place. He explored the forest surrounding the town, hunted and fished, ice-skated in the winter, sailed in the summer. In later years Hawthorne would refer to his years in Raymond as the most rewarding period of his life.

HAWTHORNE PREPARES FOR COLLEGE

On July 5, 1819, his idyllic life in Raymond came to a halt, for his mother sent him back to Salem to study in preparation for college. His education through the years had been sporadic due to his early poor health and his lack of interest; now he needed to concentrate on passing the entrance examination to Bowdoin College. In Salem he lived with his Uncle Robert, who arranged for a local lawyer to tutor him. By the summer of 1821, the tutor declared him ready to pass the entrance exam.

During those two years of study, Hawthorne found time to read *Arabian Nights*, some poetry, and books by Henry Fielding, Sir Walter Scott, Jean-Jacques Rousseau, and Caleb Williams. He also began to write. His first essays and poems were humorous, sometimes satirical. In a letter to his mother in the spring of 1821, he broached the subject of his career. After dismissing the ministry, law, and medicine, he told her that he was thinking about becoming a writer. Although the letter had a humorous tone, Hawthorne was undoubtedly serious.

PREPARATION FOR THE WRITER'S LIFE

In October 1821, accompanied by Uncle Robert (who was paying for his education), Hawthorne reported to Bowdoin College in Brunswick, Maine. He and his uncle had chosen Bowdoin because its fees were low and it was located in Maine. Hawthorne's expenses for the first term of a three-term school year totaled $19.61. He ate his meals at the home of a faculty member for an additional two dollars a week, and he paid one dollar a cord for wood to heat his room.

Offered no electives, students at Bowdoin followed a strict curriculum: Greek, Latin, mathematics, and philosophy were the major courses. The sciences, religion, and English composition received less emphasis. Hawthorne did best in the two courses he liked the most, Latin and English composition. In other courses he managed a passing grade. Because he did not like declamation (public speaking), he neglected and sometimes ignored the assignments. When he paid his fees each term, he was often assessed a fine, usually fifty cents, for not participating in declamation. Over the four years at Bowdoin, he also paid fines for skipping classes, gambling (playing cards for money), and failing to attend religious services.

The extracurricular activity that Hawthorne enjoyed most at Bowdoin was the Athenean Society, a literary club. He and his fellow Atheneans read widely and contributed many of their own books to the society's library.

Some of Hawthorne's classmates—Horatio Bridge, for example—later suggested that Hawthorne had done some writing while he was at Bowdoin, although no proof has been found. Literary historians speculate that during his senior year Hawthorne probably began his first novel, *Fanshawe*, and possibly *Seven Tales of My Native Land*. Certainly when he graduated in 1825, ranking eighteenth in a graduating class of thirty-eight, he had a solid foundation in Latin literature and English composition, the prerequisites for serious writing.

TWELVE YEARS OF ISOLATION

By the time Hawthorne finished college, his mother had moved back to Salem to live in her deceased father's home. Hawthorne returned there, too, and turned an attic room into a bedroom-study. From 1825 to 1837, he spent much of his time reading rental library books, which he studied and analyzed for their writing qualities, and writing his own works. Almost every day he wrote in the morning, then went for a solitary walk in the afternoon, usually along the seashore. Because he had been gone from Salem for several years, he knew few residents and seldom attempted to make acquaintances. He read, he wrote, and he walked.

Although Hawthorne destroyed much of his early writing, in 1828 he did anonymously self-publish his first novel, *Fanshawe*, about life in a small college. Not satisfied with the book, he soon withdrew it from circulation and asked friends to destroy their copies. As a result, extant copies are rare and extremely valuable. He also finished *Seven Tales of My Native Land*, but when the collection did not sell, he burned most of the tales. Over the years he burned manuscripts whenever they did not satisfy his expectations or when publishers refused them.

TALES FOR MAGAZINES AND JOURNALS FOR HIMSELF

Publishers did not refuse all of his work. In 1830 the editor of the Boston *Token*, an annual collection of short works, bought four of Hawthorne's tales: "The Gentle Boy," "The Wives of the Dead," "Roger Malvin's Funeral," and "My Kinsman, Major Molineux." Eventually the *Token* published more than twenty of Hawthorne's stories, and several more appeared in the *New England Magazine.* Up to 1837, however, none of his work came out under his name; the author listed was always "Anonymous" or a pseudonym. Hawthorne was doing hackwork pieces for the money at the time, and he did not want to claim them publicly.

Hawthorne also wrote in a daily journal during his twelve years of self-imposed isolation. His friend Bridge indicated that Hawthorne had started keeping a journal at Bowdoin; if so, it has not survived. The earliest extant journals date from 1837, according to Randall Stewart, Brown University professor and Hawthorne scholar. Hawthorne's journals are important because they describe his experiences, scenes he witnessed, people he met or saw, ideas for stories, and trips he took. Hawthorne biographer Mark Van Doren considers the journals "a reservoir from which he could expect to draw matter for his romances." Hawthorne did not edit entries, so the journals also reveal the progression and refinement of his style of writing.

In *The Portable Hawthorne,* editor Malcolm Cowley includes a passage from Hawthorne's 1844–1846 journal: "The life of a woman, who, by the old colony law, was condemned always to wear the letter *A,* sewed on her garment, in token of her having committed adultery." From the 1847–1849 journal, Cowley quotes another line: "A story of the effects of revenge, in diabolizing [corrupting or making evil] him who indulges in it." These two passages would have focused Hawthorne's thoughts on *The Scarlet Letter.*

HAWTHORNE PUBLISHES *TWICE-TOLD TALES*

Proof that Hawthorne's writing style was maturing came in 1837, when he published *Twice-Told Tales,* a collection of stories, some new, some he had published earlier in magazines. Bowdoin classmate Henry Wadsworth Longfellow gave *Twice-Told Tales* an enthusiastic review, but sales were only moderate. Some readers thought that Hawthorne's moralizing was a little heavy-handed. He continued to publish tales in *Token, American Monthly, Southern Rose, Godey's,* and other magazines. On the average, he received twenty-five to thirty-five dollars for each published story.

Hawthorne Meets Sophia Peabody

In the spring of 1838 Hawthorne found another reason to work hard at his writing: He met Sophia Peabody, daughter of a local dentist. Sophia and her two sisters were enthusiastically interested in the arts. Because Hawthorne was a handsome, genial man, other young girls had found him attractive, but Sophia won his heart. They became secretly engaged in 1839, and remained so for three years. They vowed that before they could marry, Sophia, whose chronic headaches kept her a semi-invalid, had to get stronger and healthier, and Hawthorne had to earn enough money to support a wife.

A Political Appointment

His friends Horatio Bridge and Franklin Pierce offered to help Hawthorne find a job. They had tried unsuccessfully earlier to get him a political appointment. This time their contacts with members of the Democratic Party were productive, and Hawthorne was appointed the measurer of salt and coal in the Boston Custom-House at a salary of fifteen hundred dollars a year. For the two years that Hawthorne held this position, from 1839 to 1841, he had time to write only letters to Sophia back in Salem.

At first he liked the job because he was meeting new, interesting people. But eventually the rigors of the job became too much for Hawthorne. He was required outdoors on the wharf and on and off boats in all kinds of weather. The days were long, and he returned to his room at night exhausted and covered with coal dust. On January 1, 1841, he resigned to live in an experimental utopian community called Brook Farm, where he hoped he and Sophia could live. He did his share of farm work during the day, but found he was far too tired in the evening to pick up his pen to write. When Sophia came for a visit, she noticed immediately that he seemed to be more an observer than a participant. Conceding that she was right, he admitted that Brook Farm was not for him, after all. Feeling obligated to help harvest the year's crops, however, he stayed until fall. In October 1841 he returned to Salem.

Realizing that writing was his one resource, Hawthorne declared that he would concentrate on only that. Magazines offered the quickest chance for income, so he went to Albany to settle the rate of pay with the editor of *Democratic Review.*

Apparently having reached a satisfactory agreement, he returned to Salem confident and hopeful.

MARRIAGE AND A MOVE TO CONCORD

Hawthorne was so sure that his affairs were going to improve that he decided he and Sophia should not wait any longer to marry. Sophia was in good health. Reluctant at first, his mother and his sisters had come to accept his marrying. All signs were positive. On July 9, 1842, after a wedding at her parents' home, Hawthorne and his bride immediately took a carriage to a rented property recently available in Concord, the Old Manse.

Apparently Hawthorne and Sophia were fully as happy as they had expected to be. He settled into a routine of writing for magazines in the morning and walking and reading in the afternoon. He became friendly with the literary men of Concord who were known as Transcendentalists—Emerson, Thoreau, Alcott, and Channing. Always on good terms with these writers, the affable Hawthorne nevertheless remained somewhat aloof. Hawthorne could never open himself completely to anyone, except perhaps Sophia.

Although Hawthorne continued to write for magazines, he was finding the struggle to pay the family's bills increasingly difficult. The magazine editors were slow to pay him for the stories that they published. The birth of the Hawthornes' first daughter, Una, brought them joy and pride and more bills. When the owner of the Old Manse decided to return to the house, Hawthorne and Sophia had to move in with his mother and sisters in Salem.

HAWTHORNE'S FRIENDS COME TO HIS AID

Unable to support his family by writing, in 1845 Hawthorne again had to ask Bridge and Pierce for help in finding a job. Not until April 3, 1846, were the two able to get Hawthorne appointed surveyor for the district of Salem and inspector of revenue for the port of Salem. He would earn twelve hundred dollars a year, enough to start paying his debts and support his family. This security was a relief, especially when his son, Julian, was born in June 1846. As an added bonus, he managed to publish *Mosses from an Old Manse*, a collection of twenty-five of some of his best short stories, including "Young Goodman Brown," "The Birthmark," and "Rappaccini's Daughter."

Hawthorne's respite from money worries was short-lived, however. The Whigs won the presidential election of 1848, which meant Democratic political appointees would lose their jobs, and Hawthorne was a Democrat. He decided to fight to keep his job, but the spoils system prevailed; on June 8, 1848, Hawthorne was officially dismissed.

HAWTHORNE BEGINS *THE SCARLET LETTER*

Hawthorne began writing again, and finances were still tight. Sophia surprised him by revealing that she had been saving some money each week from her household allowance. To help more, she began making lampshades and screens to sell. And friends sent money; not all of the donors are known, but Longfellow was among them.

Hawthorne began work on a novel that he had long wanted to write, centered on a man who is ruled by his intelligence rather than by his heart. As if obsessed, Hawthorne began the book he would call *The Scarlet Letter;* he wrote so steadily and so furiously that he became ill with exhaustion.

Eventually hearing of Hawthorne's illness, an acquaintance, James Fields of publishers Ticknor and Fields, paid a call. Trying to encourage Hawthorne, Fields told him that he should begin publishing again. When Fields asked him what he was working on, Hawthorne just shook his head. As Fields was leaving, Hawthorne suddenly called for him to wait. Shortly he came downstairs and handed Fields a not-quite-finished version of *The Scarlet Letter*.

Hawthorne had incorporated many old characters from his previous writings into the book. The 1837 edition of *Twice-Told Tales* includes the forebears of two *Scarlet Letter* characters. In "Endicott and the Red Cross," standing among the victims being punished by the Puritans is a young woman wearing a capital *A* on the front of her gown—a model for Hester. Chillingworth descends from Ethan Brand, the main character in a story by the same name. Brand sacrifices his humanity for intelligence, as Chillingworth would sacrifice his humanity for revenge. Dimmesdale, the young idealist who cannot survive in this world, is in several of Hawthorne's tales under different names. Hawthorne had also investigated the themes of *The Scarlet Letter* before: hidden guilt; the intelligent, unfeeling heart; and the inability to confess one's wrongdoing. Hawthorne brought them all together in his masterpiece. His own strain of despair dictated the ending of *The Scarlet Letter:* One cannot expiate one's own sins. Chillingworth and Dimmesdale both die; Pearl gives Hester an escape to England, but Hester voluntarily returns to Boston, sews the scarlet *A* on her gown again, and resumes her punishment. Even in death she is still being punished, for her tombstone bears the inscription "On a Field, Sable, the Letter A, Gules" (on a black field, a red letter *A*).

THE SCARLET LETTER IS A SUCCESS

Ticknor and Fields published *The Scarlet Letter* on March 16, 1850. The book was an immediate success. But in Salem, "The Custom-House," the autobiographical introduction, drew an emphatically negative response. The townspeople disputed Hawthorne's unflattering descriptions of some of the "regulars" at the Custom-House. When the publisher issued a second edition two weeks later, Hawthorne, mindful of the wrath of the Salem readers, reconsidered his comments. He wrote a second preface, in which he acknowledged and defended his earlier comments, and he ended with "The author is constrained, therefore, to republish his introductory sketch without the change of a word." The people of Salem were unappeased. Nonetheless, although Hawthorne himself never did fully comprehend that he had written a masterpiece, the work garnered immediate high praise.

In May 1850 the ever-restless Hawthornes moved to an old farmhouse in Lenox, Massachusetts. That summer, Hawthorne met Herman Melville, who lived nearby, and the two liked each other immediately. As always, Hawthorne kept slightly aloof; Melville was more open in his admiration for Hawthorne, to whom he dedicated his masterpiece, *Moby-Dick.* In the fall, Hawthorne began working on another romance, *The House of Seven Gables.*

In 1851 Hawthorne and Sophia moved to West Newton, Massachusetts, where their third child, Rose, was born. Here Hawthorne finished writing and published *The House of the Seven Gables,* in which he considers the effects of one man's sin upon succeeding generations. In the preface he stated the moral of the book: "The wrong-doing of one generation lives into the successive ones, and divesting itself of every temporary advantage, becomes a pure and uncontrollable mischief." That year he also published his first book for children, *True Stories from History and Biography.* With his knowledge of history, Hawthorne quickly and easily retold these events in a suitable manner for children.

In 1852 the Hawthornes moved into their newly purchased house, Wayside, in Concord. There he wrote *The Blithedale Romance*, which tells the story of life in a community much like Brook Farm. Hyatt Waggoner, in his study of Hawthorne, suggests that Blithedale is "blithe dale," or a happy valley. If so, the title is misleading, for the happy valley ends as a fool's paradise. In 1852 Hawthorne published *A Wonder Book for Boys and Girls*, a retelling of classical myths, as well as a political biography of his friend Franklin Pierce, who had just been elected president of the United States. In 1853 Hawthorne produced *Tanglewood Tales*, the retelling of six more Greek myths.

THE HAWTHORNES LIVE ABROAD

Although Hawthorne had been publishing regularly, he was not as financially secure as he wanted to be. When President Pierce appointed him consul at Liverpool, England, in 1853, Hawthorne thought his situation was relieved. As consul, an official who supervised the commercial interests of the United States in England, Hawthorne would get a regular, predictable income. Though the post was not lucrative enough to make him financially secure, he was able to observe some of England's cultural richness. Hawthorne was especially impressed with England's great cathedrals, which he visited regularly. At an art museum one day he saw poet Alfred Tennyson; characteristically Hawthorne watched Tennyson from a distance, but did not approach him.

When Pierce was not reelected in 1857, Hawthorne was dismissed as consul. He and Sophia traveled to Italy and lived in Florence and Rome while he wrote *The Marble Faun*. He chose Rome as the setting for this fourth romance, thus enabling him to enrich the book with descriptions of the exciting atmosphere and art of that cosmopolitan city. *The Marble Faun* tells the story of a man who commits a murder, but later realizes the seriousness of his crime, repents, and confesses to the authorities. In this case, the protagonist grows in moral stature as a result of his sin.

In 1860 Hawthorne and Sophia returned to Wayside. In failing health, he wrote one more book, *Our Old Home*, published in 1863, a collection of sketches about life in England. On May 19, 1864, Pierce took him on a short trip in an effort to revive his spirits. That night they shared adjoining rooms at a Plymouth, New Hampshire, inn. Pierce awakened during the night and looked through the open door between their rooms to see Hawthorne lying in exactly the same position he had taken on retiring. Pierce checked his friend and found that Hawthorne had died. He was buried in Sleepy Hollow Cemetery in Concord.

CHAPTER 1

Structure and Style in *The Scarlet Letter*

READINGS ON
THE SCARLET LETTER

A Powerful Masterpiece

Mark Van Doren

Literary critic and author Mark Van Doren writes
about the enduring power and drama inherent in
The Scarlet Letter. Van Doren believes that the book's
discussion of human consciences and differences
makes it relevant to people today.

Hawthorne did not need to believe in Puritanism in order to
write a great novel about it. He had only to understand it,
which for a man of his time was harder. If it was not impossible for him, the reason is less his experience than his genius, and the fact that something of supreme importance
had survived in his lonely thought. He was so alone, so aloof,
because he found so few around him whose seriousness
equaled his; and by seriousness he meant the real thing, a
thing consistent with irony and love, a thing indeed for
which comedy might be as suitable an expression as
tragedy. If one were serious, one never forgot the eternal importance of every soul, and never doubted that the consequences of deeds, even of impulses, last forever. The Puritans had known this all too well, and their resulting
behavior was at times abominable. *The Scarlet Letter* is say-
ing so at the same time that it is revealing a world where
tragedy and comedy are possible.

The conflict in Hawthorne of two worlds between which
he hung, exposing the fanaticism of one, despising the
blandness of the other, is not the least source of *The Scarlet Letter*'s power. The book was and is a reminder to modern man, who still talks about his conscience, of where that
conscience came from. For Hawthorne it came from a dark
world where human injustice was done, but only because
men fumbled in their understanding of justice. Justice itself was a form of fate; or, for Hawthorne, so it must seem
to any mortal and therefore limited intelligence. To any
man "the rickety machine and crazy action of the uni-

Excerpted from *Nathaniel Hawthorne* by Mark Van Doren (New York: William Sloane
Associates, 1949). Copyright ©1949 by William Sloane Associates, Inc. All rights reserved. Reprinted by permission of the author's estate.

verse" must appear all but incomprehensible, as at times it did to Hester Prynne. . . .

THE SCARLET LETTER IS A TRAGEDY

For such an imagination the drama of guilt did not lose its drama by being terrible. As an artist he was committed to drama; which was why he could see so clearly the differences between men. He saw these differences in terms of the evil they did or did not recognize—did recognize, and so were warm in peace; did not, and so were merciless to those for whom concealment was impossible, or else were corrupted by the suppression involved in evil's "turning its poison back among the inner vitalities" of their souls. For such an imagination also there was no social gospel, of Brook Farm or of any other place, that could serve as a substitute for the simple act of recognizing that every soul, beginning with one's own, is sadly imperfect. Hester does good deeds, but in themselves they are not enough; they do not give her mind the rest it desires. In "The Custom House" Hawthorne even wonders whether the compulsion to do them had not made her at times "an intruder and a nuisance."

Out of such ideas as these, possessed for once by Hawthorne in the available form of a perfect balance, the force of *The Scarlet Letter* surely derives. He was an artist, and so he knew how to use the ideas; but it would be wrong to deny that he had them, as Henry James substantially does when he discovers in Hawthorne "no general views in the least uncomfortable." Hawthorne's "general views" were so serious, so profound, that they left him free to write a tragedy. Duplicity is not denounced in Dimmesdale; it is comprehended, and so made terrible. If the views of Hawthorne did not extend to the understanding that the isolation of modern man—so much more awful than the solitude of the Puritan who at least was alone with God—is an isolation for which no cure exists, we have perhaps the reason for his failure to equal *The Scarlet Letter* in any subsequent effort. It was written, we may admit, with more feeling than thought—though with the deepest and most delicate feeling. We need not suppose, however, that it was done with tricks.

A MASTERPIECE

The structure of the tale is justly celebrated, and its economy, and its lighting—"densely dark," says James, "with a single spot of vivid color in it." That spot is not the letter A alone; it is the meaning this letter keeps, and the power it has to illuminate the soul of Hester Prynne. We see her with it at the start, stationary on the scaffold, and we see her beneath it at the close, stationary in her grave. The story moves rapidly, as fate moves, but through a series of tableaux in which everything seems to stand still. . . .

The Scarlet Letter, like any masterpiece, is powerful everywhere and all the time. If its scene is bleak, itself is blended of the richest, most moving, most splendid things, put densely and inseparably together.

Flaws in
The Scarlet Letter

Henry James

The major American writer and literary critic Henry
James critiques *The Scarlet Letter* in his book *Hawthorne*—the first comprehensive study ever written
about an American author.

James was seven years old when Hawthorne published *The Scarlet Letter.* He vaguely remembered
the flurry of excitement the novel had aroused
among his book-loving family and their friends.
When he read the book as an adult and as a writer
himself, he readily judged it a masterpiece. However,
he did find several flaws, which he listed in detail.

[*The Scarlet Letter*] has the tone of the circumstances in
which it was produced. If Hawthorne was in a sombre mood,
and if his future were painfully vague, *The Scarlet Letter*
contains little enough of gaiety or of hopefulness. It is
densely dark, with a single spot of vivid colour in it; and it
will probably long remain the most consistently gloomy of
English novels of the first order. But I ... called it the author's masterpiece, and I imagine it will continue to be, for
other generations than ours, his most substantial title to
fame. The subject had probably lain a long time in his mind,
as his subjects were apt to do; so that he appears completely
to possess it, to know it and feel it. It is simpler and more
complete than his other novels; it achieves more perfectly
what it attempts, and it has about it that charm, very hard to
express, which we find in an artist's work the first time he
has touched his highest mark—a sort of straightness and
naturalness of execution, an unconsciousness of his public,
and freshness of interest in his theme. It was a great success,
and he immediately found himself famous. The writer of
these lines, who was a child at the time, remembers dimly

Excerpted from *Hawthorne* by Henry James (London: Macmillan, 1879).

the sensation the book produced, and the little shudder with which people alluded to it, as if a peculiar horror were mixed with its attractions. . . .

AMERICA'S FIRST NOTEWORTHY NOVEL

Hawthorne himself was very modest about it; he wrote to his publisher, when there was a question of his undertaking another novel, that what had given the history of Hester Prynne its "vogue" was simply the introductory chapter. In fact, the publication of *The Scarlet Letter* was in the United States a literary event of the first importance. The book was the finest piece of imaginative writing yet put forth in the country. There was a consciousness of this in the welcome that was given it—a satisfaction in the idea of America having produced a novel that belonged to literature, and to the forefront of it. Something might at last be sent to Europe as exquisite in quality as anything that had been received, and the best of it was that the thing was absolutely American; it belonged to the soil, to the air; it came out of the very heart of New England.

It is beautiful, admirable, extraordinary; it has in the highest degree that merit which I have spoken of as the mark of Hawthorne's best things—an indefinable purity and lightness of conception, a quality which in a work of art affects one in the same way as the absence of grossness does in a human being. His fancy, as I just now said, had evidently brooded over the subject for a long time; the situation to be represented had disclosed itself to him in all its phases. When I say in all its phases, the sentence demands modification; for it is to be remembered that if Hawthorne laid his hand upon the well-worn theme, upon the familiar combination of the wife, the lover, and the husband, it was, after all, but to one period of the history of these three persons that he attached himself. The situation is the situation after the woman's fault has been committed, and the current of expiation and repentance has set in. In spite of the relation between Hester Prynne and Arthur Dimmesdale, no story of love was surely ever less of a "love-story." To Hawthorne's imagination the fact that these two persons had loved each other too well was of an interest comparatively vulgar; what appealed to him was the idea of their moral situation in the long years that were to follow. The story, indeed, is in a secondary degree that of Hester Prynne; she becomes, really, after the first scene, an accessory figure; it is not upon her the *dénoûment* depends. It is upon her guilty lover that the author projects most frequently the cold, thin rays of his fitfully-moving lantern, which makes here and there a little luminous circle, on the edge of which hovers the livid and sinister figure of the injured and retributive husband. The story goes on, for the most part, between the lover and the husband—the tormented young Puritan minister, who carries the secret of his own lapse from pastoral purity locked up beneath an exterior that commends itself to the reverence of his flock, while he sees the softer partner of his guilt standing in the full glare of exposure and humbling herself to the misery of atonement—between this more wretched and pitiable culprit, to whom dishonour would come as a comfort and the pillory as a relief, and the older, keener, wiser man, who, to obtain satisfaction for the wrong he has suffered, devises the infernally ingenious plan of conjoining himself with his wronger, living with him, living upon him; and while he pretends to minister to his hidden ailment and to sympathise with his pain, revels in his unsuspected knowledge of these things, and stimulates them by malignant arts. The attitude of Roger Chillingworth, and the means he takes to compensate himself—these are the highly original elements in the situation that Hawthorne so ingeniously treats. None of his works are so impregnated with that after-sense of the old Puritan consciousness of life to which allusion has so often been made. . . .

THE BOOK DOES HAVE FAULTS

The story happens to be of so-called historical cast, to be told of the early days of Massachusetts, and of people in steeple-crowned hats and sad-coloured garments. The historical colouring is rather weak than otherwise; there is little elaboration of detail, of the modern realism of research; and the author has made no great point of causing his figures to speak the English of their period. Nevertheless, the book is full of the moral presence of the race that invented Hester's penance—diluted and complicated with other things, but still perfectly recognisable. Puritanism, in a word, is there, not only objectively, as Hawthorne tried to place it there, but subjectively as well. Not, I mean, in his judgment of his characters in any harshness of prejudice, or in the obtrusion of a moral lesson; but in the very quality of his own vision, in the tone of the picture, in a certain coldness and exclusiveness of treatment.

The faults of the book are, to my sense, a want of reality and an abuse of the fanciful element—of a certain superficial symbolism. The people strike me not as characters, but as representatives, very picturesquely arranged, of a single state of mind; and the interest of the story lies, not in them, but in the situation, which is insistently kept before us, with little progression, though with a great deal, as I have said, of a certain stable variation; and to which they, out of their reality, contribute little that helps it to live and move. . . .

Too Much Symbolism?

In *The Scarlet Letter* there is a great deal of symbolism; there is, I think, too much. It is overdone at times, and becomes mechanical; it ceases to be impressive, and grazes triviality. The idea of the mystic A which the young minister finds imprinted upon his breast and eating into his flesh, in sympathy with the embroidered badge that Hester is condemned to wear, appears to me to be a case in point. This suggestion should, I think, have been just made and dropped; to insist upon it and return to it, is to exaggerate the weak side of the subject. Hawthorne returns to it constantly, plays with it, and seems charmed by it; until at last the reader feels tempted to declare that his enjoyment of it is puerile [childish]. In the admirable scene, so superbly conceived and beautifully executed, in which Mr. Dimmesdale, in the stillness of the night, in the middle of the sleeping town, feels impelled to go and stand upon the scaffold where his mistress had formerly enacted her dreadful penance, and then, seeing Hester pass along the street, from watching at a sickbed, with little Pearl at her side, calls them both to come and stand there beside him—in this masterly episode the effect is almost spoiled by the introduction of one of these superficial conceits. What leads up to it is very fine—so fine that I cannot do better than quote it as a specimen of one of the striking pages of the book.

> But before Mr. Dimmesdale had done speaking, a light gleamed far and wide over all the muffled sky. It was doubtless caused by one of those meteors which the night-watcher may so often observe burning out to waste in the vacant regions of the atmosphere. So powerful was its radiance that it thoroughly illuminated the dense medium of cloud betwixt the sky and earth. The great vault brightened, like the dome of

an immense lamp. It showed the familiar scene of the street with the distinctness of mid-day, but also with the awfulness that is always imparted to familiar objects by an unaccustomed light. The wooden houses, with their jutting stories and quaint gable-peaks; the doorsteps and thresholds, with the early grass springing up about them; the garden-plots, black with freshly-turned earth; the wheel-track, little worn, and, even in the market-place, margined with green on either side;—all were visible, but with a singularity of aspect that seemed to give another moral interpretation to the things of this world than they had ever borne before. And there stood the minister, with his hand over his heart; and Hester Prynne, with the embroidered letter glimmering on her bosom; and little Pearl herself a symbol, and the connecting link between these two. They stood in the noon of that strange and solemn splendour, as if it were the light that is to reveal all secrets, and the daybreak that shall unite all that belong to one another.

That is imaginative, impressive, poetic; but when, almost immediately afterwards, the author goes on to say that "the minister looking upward to the zenith, beheld there the appearance of an immense letter—the letter A—marked out in lines of dull red light," we feel that he goes too far, and is in danger of crossing the line that separates the sublime from its intimate neighbour. We are tempted to say that this is not moral tragedy, but physical comedy. In the same way, too much is made of the intimation that Hester's badge had a scorching property, and that if one touched it one would immediately withdraw one's hand. Hawthorne is perpetually looking for images which shall place themselves in picturesque correspondence with the spiritual facts with which he is concerned, and of course the search is of the very essence of poetry. But in such a process discretion is everything, and when the image becomes importunate it is in danger of seeming to stand for nothing more serious than itself. . . .

AN EXCELLENT BOOK NONETHELESS

I had not meant, however, to expatiate upon his defects, which are of the slenderest and most venial kind. *The Scarlet Letter* has the beauty and harmony of all original and complete conceptions, and its weaker spots, whatever they are, are not of its essence; they are mere light flaws and inequalities of surface. One can often return to it; it supports familiarity, and has the inexhaustible charm and mystery of great works of art. It is admirably written. Hawthorne afterwards polished his style to a still higher degree; but in his later productions—it is almost always the case in a writer's later productions—there is a touch of mannerism. In *The Scarlet Letter* there is a high degree of polish, and at the same time a charming freshness; his phrase is less conscious of itself. His biographer very justly calls attention to the fact that his style was excellent from the beginning; that he appeared to have passed through no phase of learning how to write, but was in possession of his means, from the first, of his handling a pen.

Style in
The Scarlet Letter

Richard Harter Fogle

The Scarlet Letter is usually called gloomy, tense, or overly controlled. Hawthorne used several literary devices, such as dramatic irony, to avoid or at least reduce these problems. He varies the pace, relieves the tension, and/or changes the mood. Richard Harter Fogle, professor of English at the University of North Carolina, argues that Hawthorne's use of these devices prevented him from becoming too heavy-handed.

The intensity of *The Scarlet Letter*, at which Hawthorne himself was dismayed, comes from concentration, selection, and dramatic irony. The concentration upon the central theme is unremitting. The tension is lessened only once, in the scene in the forest, and then only delusively, since the hope of freedom which brings it about is quickly shown to be false and even sinful. The characters play out their tragic action against a background in itself oppressive—the somber atmosphere of Puritanism. Hawthorne calls the progression of the story "the darkening close of a tale of human frailty and sorrow." Dark to begin with, it grows steadily deeper in gloom. The method is almost unprecedentedly selective. Almost every image has a symbolic function; no scene is superfluous. One would perhaps at times welcome a loosening of the structure, a moment of wandering from the path. The weedy grassplot in front of the prison; the distorting reflection of Hester in a breastplate, where the Scarlet Letter appears gigantic; the tapestry of David and Bathsheba on the wall of the minister's chamber; the little brook in the forest; the slight malformation of Chillingworth's shoulder; the ceremonial procession on election day—in every instance more is meant than meets the eye.

Excerpted from *Hawthorne's Fiction: The Light and the Dark* by Richard Harter Fogle (Norman: University of Oklahoma Press, 1964). Copyright ©1964 by the University of Oklahoma Press, Publishing Division of the University. Reprinted by permission.

The intensity of *The Scarlet Letter* comes in part from a sustained and rigorous dramatic irony, or irony of situation. This irony arises naturally from the theme of "secret sin," or concealment. "Show freely of your worst," says Hawthorne; the action of *The Scarlet Letter* arises from the failure of Dimmesdale and Chillingworth to do so. The minister hides his sin, and Chillingworth hides his identity. This concealment affords a constant drama. There is the irony of Chapter III, "The Recognition," in which Chillingworth's ignorance is suddenly and blindingly reversed. Separated from his wife by many vicissitudes, he comes upon her as she is dramatically exposed to public infamy. From his instantaneous decision, symbolized by the lifting of his finger to his lips to hide his tie to her, he precipitates the further irony of his sustained hypocrisy.

In the same chapter Hester is confronted with her fellow-adulterer, who is publicly called upon to persuade her as her spiritual guide to reveal his identity. Under the circumstances the situation is highly charged, and his words have a double meaning—one to the onlookers, another far different to Hester and the speaker himself. " 'If thou feelest it to be for thy soul's peace, and that thy earthly punishment will therefore be made more effectual to salvation, I charge thee to speak out the name of thy fellow-sinner and fellow-sufferer!' ". . .

AMBIGUITY RELIEVES THE TENSION

[The] qualities of concentration, selectivity, and irony, which are responsible for the intensity of *The Scarlet Letter*, tend at their extreme toward excessive regularity and a sense of over-manipulation, although irony is also a counteragent against them. This tendency toward regularity is balanced by Hawthorne's use of ambiguity. The distancing of the story in the past has the effect of ambiguity. Hawthorne so employs the element of time as to warn us that he cannot guarantee the literal truth of his narrative and at the same time to suggest that the essential truth is the clearer; as facts shade off into the background, meaning is left in the foreground unshadowed and disencumbered. The years, he pretends, have winnowed his material, leaving only what is enduring. Tradition and superstition, while he disclaims belief in them, have a way of pointing to truth.

Thus the imagery of hell-fire which occurs throughout *The Scarlet Letter* is dramatically proper to the Puritan background and is attributed to the influence of superstitious legend. It works as relief from more serious concerns and still functions as a symbol of psychological and religious truth. In Chapter III, as Hester is returned from the scaffold to the prison, "It was whispered, by those who peered after her, that the scarlet letter threw a lurid gleam along the dark passage-way of the interior." The imagery of the letter may be summarized by quoting a later passage:

> The vulgar, who, in those dreary old times, were always contributing a grotesque horror to what interested their imaginations, had a story about the scarlet letter which we might readily work up into a terrific legend. They averred, that the symbol was not mere scarlet cloth, tinged in an earthly dyepot, but was red-hot with infernal fire, and could be seen glowing all alight, whenever Hester Prynne walked abroad in the nighttime. And we must needs say, it seared Hester's bosom so deeply, that perhaps there was more truth in the rumor than our modern incredulity may be inclined to admit.

The lightness of Hawthorne's tone lends relief and variety, while it nevertheless reveals the function of the superstition. "The vulgar," "dreary old times," "grotesque horror," "work up into a terrific legend"—his scorn is so heavily accented that it discounts itself and satirizes the "modern incredulity" of his affected attitude. The playful extravagance of "red-hot with infernal fire" has the same effect. And the apparent begrudging of the concession in the final sentence—"And we must needs say"—lends weight to a truth so reluctantly admitted. . . .

PURITANS: SEVERE BUT HUMAN

There is also the ambivalence of the Puritans. It is easy to pass them by too quickly. One's first impression is doubtless, as Hawthorne says elsewhere, of a set of "dismal wretches," but they are more than this. The Puritan code is arrogant, inflexible, overrighteous; and it is remarked of their magistrates and priests that "out of the whole human family, it would not have been easy to select the same number of wise and virtuous persons, who should be less capable of sitting in judgment on an erring woman's heart. . . ." Nevertheless, after finishing *The Scarlet Letter* one might well ask what merely human society would be better. With all its rigors, the ordeal of Hester upon the scaffold is invested with awe by the real seriousness and simplicity of the onlookers. Hawthorne compares the Puritan attitude, and certainly not unfavorably, to "the heartlessness of another social state, which would find only a theme for jest in an exhibition like the present." And it is counted as a virtue that the chief men of the town attend the spectacle without loss of dignity. Without question they take upon themselves more of the judgment of the soul than is fitting for men to assume, but this fault is palliated by their complete sincerity. They are "a people amongst whom religion and law were almost identical, and in whose character both were so thoroughly interfused, that the mildest and the severest acts of public discipline were alike made venerable and awful." By any ideal standard they are greatly lacking, but among erring humans they are, after all, creditable.

Furthermore, the vigor of Hawthorne's abuse of them is not to be taken at face value. They are grim, grisly, stern-browed and unkindly visaged; amid the gaiety of election day "for the space of a single holiday, they appeared scarcely more grave than most other communities at a period of general affliction." In this statement the tone of good-humored mockery is unmistakable. Hawthorne's attacks have something of the quality of a family joke; their roughness comes from thorough and even affectionate understanding. As his excellent critic and son-in-law G.P. Lathrop long ago pointed out, Hawthorne is talking of his own people and in hitting at them is quite conscious that he hits himself.

Finally, the pervasive influence of Hawthorne's style modifies the rigorous and purposeful direction of the action and the accompanying symmetrical ironies. The style is urbane, relaxed, and reposeful and is rarely without some touch of amiable and unaccented humor. This quality varies, of course, with the situation. Hester exposed on the scaffold and Dimmesdale wracked by Chillingworth are not fit subjects for humor. Yet Hawthorne always preserves a measure of distance, even at his most sympathetic. The effect of Hawthorne's prose comes partly from generality, in itself a factor in maintaining distance, as if the author at his most searching chose always to preserve a certain reticence, to keep to what is broadly representative and conceal the personal and particular. Even the most anguished emotion is clothed with decency and measure, and the most painful situations are softened by decorum.

The Scarlet Letter Is a Romance

Roy R. Male

Hawthorne's works should be considered romances because they include aspects of both the real and the imaginary, according to Roy R. Male, professor of English at the University of Oklahoma. Hawthorne tried to probe the human heart and reveal its secrets, perhaps to open the way for its truths. Male contends that Hawthorne merged poetry and narrative to help achieve these goals.

In this predominantly masculine enterprise [writing], the role of woman has always been anomalous. The notorious ineptitude of the heroine in Western films serves as a constant reminder that in a world of movement in space, a woman was simply an encumbrance. Her alternatives were to remain behind in the ancestral homestead or to adapt herself to man's ways in the covered wagon and the squatter's hut. Without density and intrigue, there was no action possible for her in fiction except the monotonous paling and blushing that we associate with [James Fenimore] Cooper's refined heroines, the grim endurance of mannish Esther Bush in *The Prairie,* or the flamboyant marksmanship of Hurricane Nell in the dime novels. Before *The Scarlet Letter* no American writer understood the values of time, tragedy, or womanhood well enough to create a woman in fiction.

HAWTHORNE'S DEFINITION OF "ROMANCE"

Hawthorne's grasp of these values was not abstract; he understood them in his medium, which was the romance. His well-known distinction between the romance and the novel no longer possesses much critical significance, since the modern novel has assumed the "latitude, both as to its fashion and material" that Hawthorne reserved for the romance.

From *Hawthorne's Tragic Vision* by Roy R. Male. Copyright ©1957 by The University of Texas Press. Reprinted by permission of W.W. Norton & Company, Inc.

But a proper appreciation of Hawthorne's work depends upon a knowledge of his medium. To be comprehensive, a definition of Hawthorne's romance should be based not only on his explicit statements in the prefaces but also on his practice. Originally, the romance was a work written in the vernacular, a medium not so far removed from Hawthorne's as might at first appear. He sought a realm where the "actual and the imaginary" might meet, a way of expressing "the highest truths through the humblest medium of familiar words and images." What this amounts to in his accomplished work is a rare combination of poetry and fiction: poetry, in that each image functions as part of a larger design; fiction, in that the narrative is woven in a "humble texture" that preserves some degree of verisimilitude.

Hawthorne's insistence upon functional imagery accounts in part for his popularity today. The modern critical tendency toward reading fiction as poetry, emphasizing image, symbol, and allegory, often results in distortion when it is applied to novels like [Stephen Crane's] *The Red Badge of Courage*. But Hawthorne's fiction lights up when examined under this kind of intensive scrutiny. Sophia Hawthorne once remarked that her husband was "extremely scrupulous about the value and effect of every expression"; his conscious artistry, though doubtless often tacitly appreciated in the past, has only in recent years been explicitly recognized. Hawthorne knew very well the limitations of his narrative talent; he never fully appreciated his genius as a poet.

HAWTHORNE'S INSIGHT

But his real strength will never be revealed by criticism that insists solely upon image-counting or study of fictional techniques. Hawthorne possessed what one of his friends called "the awful power of insight," and his fiction remains valuable chiefly because of its penetration into the essential truths of the human heart. His one fruitful subject was the problem of moral growth. This limitation was also a great virtue, for it kept his mind free from the sort of irrelevant clutter that contaminated [Edgar Allan] Poe's fiction and much of [Walt] Whitman's poetry. When his moral imagination was not engaged, Hawthorne wrote things like "Little Daffydowndilly" and "David Swan"; when it was, even in a mere sketch like "Fancy's Show Box," he is always worth reading.

To the traditional definition of the romance as a love story

Hawthorne added a dignity that stemmed from his deep understanding of the relation between man and woman, space and time, comedy and tragedy. Each of his major romances *is* a love story in a sense that may be explained by summing up his view of the rhythms in human experience.... He penetrates into space and is a master of locomotion; the undisciplined dance of gesture and attitude is his natural mode of expression. He keeps playing new roles, wearing new uniforms, hoping to find one that will fit his inner self. In short, his angle of vision is essentially protestant, revolutionary, and spatial; when fully informed, it is an attitude that is crucially important for changing men's minds....

As "love stories," Hawthorne's romances are centered upon the Original Sin. For it seems clear that he interpreted the Original Sin as the mutual love of man and woman. The most explicit evidence for this view is to be found in "The Maypole of Merry Mount." Edith and Edgar (their jarring, fluffy names are a sign of the tale's early composition) discover that "from the moment that they truly loved, they had subjected themselves to earth's doom of care and sorrow, and troubled joy, and had no more a home at Merry Mount. That was Edith's mystery." This simple statement is expanded, tested, and reiterated in later works, from *The Scarlet Letter* to *The Marble Faun.* The union of man and woman depends upon a rending of their original relation to the parent and upon a partial inversion of their natural roles. The woman must become curious about man's province of knowledge; the man must become passionately attracted to the woman and through this attraction become involved with time, sin, and suffering. The fruit of their union will be, like Pearl, at once a token of sin and a promise of redemption....

In the profound symmetrical structure of *The Scarlet Letter* we see the given elements of the moral situation. There is the woman, wedded to guilt yet offering eventual beatitude to the man if they will both accept, undeceived, her tragic promise and find the "oneness of their being" in Pearl. There is the man, involved through his passion with woman and thus with guilt—involved, that is, with life and the inexorable flow of time. So long as he avoids full commitment, his grip upon the intellectual tradition is encased in a false glove; he preaches the word, but it is hollow, without the vision, the life. And there are two masterly personifications: Pearl, the precocious offspring of the sin and thus the visible

embodiment of the inscrutable truth, and Roger Chillingworth, the image of guilt.

In *The Scarlet Letter* we see that to develop one's human
potential one must plunge into the pit in order to ascend. To
ascend the platform with Hester is to suffer the wounds, to
become involved with life and art, to sew the threads of social
responsibility. But there is also a time to rend. To ascend with
Dimmesdale is to break down the walls, to discard the hollow
glove, the old notes, the outward forms. It is to find a point of
view in which the past really enlivens and illuminates the
present. And it is to discover that the truth cannot be grasped
abstractly, that the process of knowing is ultimately consum-
mated in art and in the artistically structured life. . . .

ALLEGORY DEVELOPS THE MAIN CHARACTERS

As this summary indicates, one of my assumptions in examining the major romances is that the allegorical personifications are valuable chiefly for the way they illumine the action of the principal characters. They are not simple
personifications like Patience and Charity; they possess
enough complexity to be interesting in their own right. But
to ignore their allegorical function is to miss part of Hawthorne's charm. He was also a symbolic writer, and the
usual sharp distinction between symbolism and allegory is
not much help in interpreting his fiction. The scarlet letter,
for example, finally becomes nearly as multivalent as the
white whale in [Herman Melville's] *Moby Dick*. . . . Hawthorne shared the belief of [Ralph Waldo] Emerson and
other contemporaries that art should develop from within.
But to the expansive, somewhat shapeless tendencies inherent in the Emersonian version of the organic principle, Hawthorne opposed a rare and beautiful sense of form, of the
generic as a condition in art as in life.

This balance, the profound symmetry of his work, is not
merely a matter of technique. It expresses the tempered steel
of the man and the artist, his ability to grasp the riddle of the
Sphinx unflinchingly and humanely. Man does keep his balance by maturing in three phases, the fateful triple crossroads
of *Oedipus Rex*. His "four-legged" faunlike stance, the youthful self, is released chiefly through an act of will. Partially sev-
ering the parental bond, he discovers his identity in a group.
(For a potential author, of course, this group may be writers
in a particular literary tradition; he comes to know [Edmund]

Spenser and [John] Milton, say, as the usual college student knows his fraternity brothers.) As a result of this identification he creates a sort of magic royalty for himself; life is an Eden, a circus, a carnival. Nothing can touch him: the prophecy, the ghost, the Original Sin are buried behind him; the past and the future do not impinge upon the present.…

THE HERO WILL MATURE

American fiction is rich in examples of youths who fail to be transformed. Amasa Delano in Melville's "Benito Cereno" and Anson Hunter in [F. Scott] Fitzgerald's "The Rich Boy" come immediately to mind. More impressive are men like Ahab [in *Moby Dick*] and [Hawthorne's] Ethan Brand, who try to achieve conversion on a grand scale by the sheer force of an unchastened will, the hollowness of their hearts matched by the swelling of their rhetoric, the fiery crucible locked inside their being. Hawthorne's imagination was also engaged by the frightening possibility that passion may so overwhelm a man that he becomes welded to a vision of evil, like young Goodman Brown, or enfeebled in will, like Arthur Dimmesdale at the beginning of *The Scarlet Letter.*

The triadic stance, the perception gained in the evening of man's life, grows out of the action of his youth and the passion that ushered in his maturity. It is exactly the opposite of the first phase, except that it also depends upon an act of will. Then he needs the group to find himself; now he must detach himself from it in order to confront his own soul. Only then does he see that the very sins and aberrations that separate him from others are the one universal bond of humanity. This, I take it, is the point of [Hawthorne's] "The Minister's Black Veil." The Reverend Mr. Hooper arrives at this perception too early in his life, but it is entirely appropriate for his deathbed. A richer illustration of the rhythm of life is found at the end of *The Scarlet Letter,* where we see the man whose insights have been refined by his passion and strengthened by a newly discovered will, the child who has become humanized, and the woman who endures.

In Hawthorne's view, it is inevitable that at any given stage of life man will be somewhat askew and that he will be confronted by ambiguity and paradox. How can he rebel and accept, improvise a sermon and participate in an age-old ritual, speculate and invest at the same time? He can do so only at certain crucial moments of revelation—those epiphanies when transformation occurs. These, of course, are the high points of Hawthorne's fiction: the *Walpurgisnacht* in "Young Goodman Brown," the forest and pillory scenes in *The Scarlet Letter*, the escape of Clifford and Hepzibah from *The House of the Seven Gables*, the carnival in *The Marble Faun....*

HAWTHORNE: A ROMANCER?

The youthful will probably always consider tragedy "gloomy" and "morbid." Hawthorne must have heard this judgment of his work so often that he half-believed it to be true. The young like to keep past, present, and future in separate compartments; the complex intertwining simply confuses and unnerves them, as it did young Goodman Brown. It takes time to realize that the final mood of Hawthorne's tragedy is a tempered hopefulness, a realization that out of sin, sorrow, and decay may be born the insights, the "words of flame" uttered by Arthur Dimmesdale in the Election Sermon.

Hawthorne was not a great novelist, in the strict sense of that term. His grasp of the actual surface of life was firm but quite limited in comparison to [Charles] Dickens or [Marie-Henri Beyle] Stendhal or [Honoré de] Balzac. But, as he kept insisting, Hawthorne was a romancer. He *did* merge poetry and fiction, the imaginary and the actual, the universal and the particular. He stands midway between Dickens and Edwin Arlington Robinson in a realm of his own. Once we grasp his meanings in this unusual yet conventional medium, we recognize his absolute greatness as a writer and the centrality of his position in American literature.

A Four-Part Structure

Gordon Roper

Although some scholars believe that *The Scarlet Letter* has a three-part structure—based on the three scaffold scenes—Gordon Roper, professor emeritus of English at Trent University in Peterborough, Toronto, presents a strong case for a four-part structure. He proposes that the Puritan community, Hester, Dimmesdale, and Chillingworth are four forces that interact with one another to develop the book's main theme: the effects of sin upon the sinners.

It was in creating a form to embody his content that Hawthorne achieved an artistic success that makes *The Scarlet Letter* one of the few fine formal works of fiction in the history of the novel in English before the work of Henry James.

The form grew organically out of his intention of presenting a central theme "diversified no otherwise than by turning different sides of the same dark idea to the reader's eye." In constructing three symbolic characters to present the three different sides of the same dark idea [sin and its consequences] he had three forces to impel his narrative; by placing them in such a community as Puritan seventeenth century Boston, he had a fourth propulsive force. The technical problem now would be to build a structure that would clearly and dramatically present the three disparate sides, and yet impress upon the reader a sense of the organic interaction of the three lines of development, and finally a unity of effect for the narrative as a whole.

His solution was to build a structure in four parts. The first part focused on one force activating the other three forces; this line of action is developed to a climax wherein the dominant force loses its power to activate, and wherein incentive is provided for one of the three hitherto dominated forces to become the new activating force. The second part develops the course of this new force acting on the other

Excerpted from the Introduction to *The Scarlet Letter and Selected Prose Works* by Gordon Roper (New York: Hendricks House, 1949). Copyright ©1949 by Hendricks House–Farrar, Straus. Reprinted by permission of Gordon Roper.

three, up to a second climax, where the power to activate passes to a third force; the third part follows the same pattern and in its climax releases the fourth and final force which brings the narration to its dramatic close.

To gain dramatic effectiveness, in each part Hawthorne has focused the narrative on the conflict between the activating force and only one of the other three forces; the effect of the activating force on the remaining two dominated forces is woven into the action indirectly.

Thus in part one, Hawthorne reveals the force of the Puritan community operating on Hester, Chillingworth, and Dimmesdale. Economically, however, the action focuses on the conflict between the community and Hester. The opening chapter states the "dark idea" of the narrative in symbolic terms; Chapter II particularizes the "dark idea" in dramatic terms. Hester Prynne has sinned against the community and the community is punishing her by public isolation on the scaffold, and by isolation without its boundaries. Hester seems to submit to the action of her community but the rebellious force that is within her is suggested. In Chapter III, the force that Chillingworth embodies is introduced in muted fashion, followed in even more muted terms by the introduction of the potentialities of Dimmesdale; both of these allowed themselves to be dominated by their community without apparent opposition. Chapters V and VI define the consequences of the community's punishment on Hester in long passages of psychological analysis. Here Hester is shown, superficially conforming to the values imposed by the community, thus performing a false penance. Chapters VII and VIII bring the potential conflict between the community and Hester to a peak when the community summons Hester before them to decide whether they should deprive the mother of her child. In Chapter VIII the community forces Dimmesdale to recognize Hester as a parishioner and as her minister to plead for her and her child; his acquiescence ironically underlines his failure to come to her aid in his natural role. The community, as activator of the narrative to this point, has created an apparent stability that from their viewpoint should be maintained; consequently they cease here to be the activator in the narrative. But by their action they have made Chillingworth aware that Dimmesdale is the man he is searching for, and thus they open the way for a new force to become activator of the narrative.

In Chapter IX Hawthorne opens a second quarter of his structure in which Chillingworth is the force that acts on the other characters. Here again, as in the first quarter, Hawthorne focuses attention upon one force acting principally on only one of the other characters, subordinating, in this case, Hester and the community. Chapter IX analyzes the nature of the force Chillingworth personifies. Chapter X dramatizes Chillingworth acting upon Dimmesdale; Chapter XI analyzes the psychological reaction in Dimmesdale to the pressures Chillingworth applies. Chapter XII dramatizes these effects, reaching a climax wherein Dimmesdale is driven in order to escape his suffering, to undertake an empty penance on the scaffold in the deserted square. The minister fails to exert his own yet unregenerated force, and is led away by Chillingworth. But on the scaffold, Hawthorne has arranged an event which releases a force hitherto suppressed. By joining hands with the minister on the scaffold, Hester's full human sympathies are reawakened.

Her force is now asserted in Chapter XIII and is to dominate the narrative through this third quarter of the book. Chapter XIII analyzes this new force in Hester. Chapter XIV dramatizes the ascendancy of her force over Chillingworth's; she frees herself from his force by renouncing the vow of silence she had made to him. She then turns to act on Dimmesdale. Before she acts, Hawthorne presents another analysis of her power, and then in Chapter XVI she and Dimmesdale are brought together in the forest. Hester tries to force a reunion with him on her terms by planning that they flee the community. Dimmesdale begs her to be his strength and to act for them. He leaves the forest in Chapter XX, in a maze caused by Hester's domination. But at the conclusion of this chapter the last structural force asserts itself, and we are prepared to move into the fourth quarter of the narrative. Hester's domination over the minister is submerged as he works in the dark at his Election Sermon; apparently the regenerating hand of God descends upon him as the dawn breaks, and at last he has the strength and will to act in accord with the dictates of his spirit.

In the fourth and last quarter, Dimmesdale is the force whose actions drive the narrative to its dramatic conclusion on the scaffold. At this point the architectural skill of Hawthorne is apparent; while other quarters followed the pattern of first analyzing the force which is to dominate the quarter, here Hawthorne shifts the viewpoint back onto Hester only to show that her power to act has run out. Chapter XXIII brings her force to its lowest ebb in the entire narrative; at the same time she realizes that the force now lies in Dimmesdale. And from this lowest point in Hester, Hawthorne moves us up to the most dramatic expression of force in the narrative, the final scene on the scaffold. Here Dimmesdale's regeneration gives him the strength to reveal his sin publicly. He is reunited with Hester and Pearl; his hypocritical relation with his community is changed into a true relationship, and he dies, to be reunited with his God.

The last chapter concludes the course of Chillingworth's life; disposes of the future of the Pearl who was made human by Dimmesdale's action on the scaffold. Then in conclusion it refocuses on the pair of forces which it had dealt with as the narrative opened, Hester and her community. We are shown how they effected a compromise in her life and in her burial. She dies, still haunted by the problem of the right relationship between the sexes, which she has come to realize is not her lot to solve in her community and in her time.

Allegory in
The Scarlet Letter

David Levin

Most literary critics agree that Nathaniel Hawthorne
had an overactive sense of guilt. Having grown up in
Salem, Massachusetts, he knew the history of his ancestors, the austere Puritans who had settled there.
William Hathorne, his great-great-great grandfather,
had punished transgressors in the Salem Colony with
unreasonable severity. His great-great grandfather,
John Hathorne, was one of the infamous magistrates
at the Salem witch trials in 1692. Some literary critics, including David Levin, professor of American
literature at Stanford University and author of *What
Happened at Salem?*, suggest that Hawthorne actually
assumed the guilt of his ancestors. In *The Scarlet Letter*, Hawthorne studies not guilt itself, but the psychological effects it has on its victims.

In his discussion of this novel, Levin analyzes Hawthorne's use of allegory as an integral part of the author's writing style. He also studies Hawthorne's use
of symbolism to supplement the allegory. Although
some critics claim that *The Scarlet Letter* has no conflict, Levin claims that conflict is indeed present—the
conflict between characters' minds and their hearts.

Nathaniel Hawthorne, born in 1804 in an age that spoke
often of inevitable progress, wrote his best fiction about the
distant past. Like many other Americans of his time and our
own, he sometimes thought of his country as a land of great
promise for the hopes of all humanity, as the land of the future, and he sometimes felt embarrassed by her lack of a rich
traditional history. Yet he said that he felt haunted by memo-
ries of his seventeenth-century ancestors, one of whom had
played an important role more than 150 years earlier in con-

Excerpted from "Nathaniel Hawthorne: *The Scarlet Letter*" by David Levin, in *The
American Novel: From James Fenimore Cooper to William Faulkner*, edited by Wallace
Stegner. Copyright ©1965 by Basic Books, Inc. Reprinted by permission of BasicBooks,
a division of HarperCollins Publishers, Inc.

demning twenty people to death for witchcraft, and he studied Puritan history with a persistence that some scholars (along with Hawthorne himself) have considered obsessive.

This mixed attitude toward the present and the past led Hawthorne to confront in his best work some of the most troublesome issues in American society and to use his knowledge of history as a means of speaking to his contemporaries. In discussing *The Scarlet Letter,* I shall try to explain the value of Hawthorne's method, and I shall pay especial attention to the skill with which Hawthorne used allegory to give the English and American novel a new intensity of psychological analysis. . . .

A PSYCHOLOGICAL ROMANCE

He wrote in a time that showed a strong interest in romantic histories, grand epics in which heroic explorers or military leaders moved through sublime scenes. And he, along with thousands of his countrymen, admired the historical romances of Sir Walter Scott and James Fenimore Cooper. He was well aware of the shallow characterization in these works, but he resolved to use the conventional forms as a way of writing a new kind of fiction. Most of the popular writers of romance had been content to treat characters as stereotypes: the dashing, warm-hearted hero who was sympathetic to nature and who obeyed natural laws was pitted against a heartless, intellectual villain who defended the letter of the law. In this scheme the complexity of human character was usually suggested, not within one person, but by contrasts between other groups of simple types, such as the two heroines: the fair lady, whose moderate feelings pointed the way to true values; and the dark lady, who was either too intellectual or too passionate to be a fit mate for the hero. Hawthorne accepted such conventions and transformed them. He called his fiction *psychological romance,* and he declared that he would "burrow into the depths of our common nature." He used the historical romance and its conventions to achieve a deeper psychological intensity than any of his predecessors had accomplished. And, of course, in turning to the past, he turned to the Puritan past.

There are several reasons why this choice was remarkably appropriate. Hawthorne, like his ancestors, was preoccupied with the moral life, with questions of responsibility and motivation, and with the moral and psychological effects of sin or misfortune. He once spoke apologetically of his "inveterate habit of allegory." In writing about the Puritans he was able to bring his readers into a world of people who considered their own lives allegorical. Hawthorne believed that the romance, unlike the novel, did not have to restrict itself to the probable; so long as the romance was true to what he called the truth of the human heart, it had every right to mingle the marvelous and the real. Romances, he said, ought to be written and read by moonlight or by the dim light of the coal fire, in an atmosphere that brings the reader into "a neutral territory, somewhere between the real world and fairyland, where the actual and imaginary may meet and each imbue itself with the nature of the other." ... When Hawthorne chose to write about seventeenth-century Boston, whose people really believed in devils and witches and in a jealous God who intervened in their daily affairs, he chose a community that recognized no clear line between the real world and what we might call fairyland; he chose a community in which it was especially difficult to distinguish between the actual and the imaginary.

SIN AND ITS CONSEQUENCES

The Scarlet Letter is the story of three sinners and the consequences of their acts. The red letter "A" that the heroine is obliged to wear on her bosom represents her adultery, but as the first letter of the alphabet it may also stand for the original sin of Adam, in which Puritans believed all men participated. Children in seventeenth-century Boston had learned their alphabet from a book that printed a little verse for each letter. The first letter was illustrated by this verse:

> In Adam's fall
> We sinned all.

We all sinned with Adam, at the beginning.

HESTER, "THE PUBLICLY KNOWN SINNER"

Hawthorne's novel begins with a scene on the scaffold, in the market place of Boston, where the heroine stands in disgrace with her infant child held close as if to conceal the letter "A" on her gown. Hester Prynne, a gentlewoman whose husband is thought to be missing at sea, has borne a child fathered by another man, and she stands in disgrace before the entire community. The chief ministers of the community, including the guilty lover, Arthur Dimmesdale, admon-

ish her to reveal the name of her child's father, but she refuses. On this day of her shame, however, her husband (who
has been shipwrecked and rescued by Indians) arrives.
When he sees his wife on the scaffold, he resolves to conceal
his identity and to seek out the child's true father. He assumes the cold name of Roger Chillingworth, and he makes
his wife promise to keep his secret.

REVEALING REFLECTIONS

As shown in this excerpt from The Scarlet Letter, *when
Hester and Pearl look at the breastplate they see reflections of themselves; thus, the breastplate becomes an extension,
or a variation, of the mirror symbol. Hawthorne expands the
meaning of the symbol by having it reflect Hester's letter* A,
*"exaggerated and gigantic"—which is the way the letter has
affected her life. Pearl sees her own expression of "naughty
merriment" also enlarged, just as it is a dominating characteristic of her personality.*

Little Pearl—who was as greatly pleased with the gleaming
armour as she had been with the glittering frontispiece of the
house—spent some time looking into the polished mirror of
the breastplate.

"Mother," cried she, "I see you here. Look! Look!"

Hester looked, by way of humoring the child; and she saw
that, owing to the peculiar effect of this convex mirror, the
scarlet letter was represented in exaggerated and gigantic pro-
portions, so as to be greatly the most prominent feature of her
appearance. In truth, she seemed absolutely hidden behind it.
Pearl pointed upward, also, at a similar picture in the head-
piece; smiling at her mother, with the elfish intelligence that
was so familiar an expression on her small physiognomy.
That look of naughty merriment was likewise reflected in the
mirror, with so much breadth and intensity of effect, that it
made Hester Prynne feel as if it could not be the image of her
own child, but of an imp who was seeking to mould itself into
Pearl's shape.

From these opening scenes the novel moves inexorably to
its tragic conclusion. Hawthorne concentrates first on Hester's punishment, her suffering, and her psychological endurance during the next seven years, and then he describes
Chillingworth's determined quest for the closely guarded secret. Chillingworth, by instinct or black art, has been at-

tracted to the guilty Dimmesdale, and in the guise of physician and friend he watches for the conclusive evidence. Hawthorne shows us the guilty man's suffering from Chillingworth's point of view, and then we see the minister's full agony from inside his own mind as he struggles unsuccessfully to make a public confession.

When Hester sees how much her former lover is suffering, she resolves to protect him. She tells him of her husband's identity and persuades him to escape with her and her child to another country. But her lover's impulse toward self-destruction and his overwhelming need to confess make this hope impossible. On the day of the planned departure he delivers his last great sermon and then ascends the scaffold, before the whole community; he confesses his guilt, asks Hester's forgiveness, embraces his daughter, and dies. Chillingworth, who has renounced his name in pursuit of revenge, has no life left. Hester leaves the community but returns for penance after her daughter has grown up. The daughter Pearl, we are told by the narrator who has been reconstructing the tale from old records, seems to have married in Europe and led a happy, comfortable life after all.

Hawthorne's great achievement in this simple story is to relate the allegory of sinners and the conflict between intellect and natural emotion so that we see not only his judgment of a historical community but also his clear perception of human psychology and the human predicament in almost any community. All three sinners are isolated from humanity, but each in a different way that is related both to the allegory and to the conflict of intellect and heart. Hester Prynne is the publicly known, partially penitent sinner. Arthur Dimmesdale is the secret sinner. Roger Chillingworth is the unpardonable sinner. Let us consider these characters somewhat more carefully, to discover how Hawthorne gives his allegory the substance and complexity of human reality.

Hester Prynne, though more obviously isolated from society than either of the men, has a closer emotional relationship to humanity than either of them can establish, and she is therefore less seriously damaged. Pearl, her daughter, is the emblem of her sin but also a means of salvation—moral salvation if we accept the Christian terminology of the seventeenth century, psychological rehabilitation if we insist on the secular terminology of a later time. Love and concern for

Pearl save Hester from wandering too far in the intellectual and moral wilderness, to which her own pride and her isolation by society tempt her.

Hester's sin, by the standards of Hawthorne's romantic psychology, is excessive passion; because it is a *natural* transgression, an expression of her vital energy, she is stronger than either Dimmesdale or Chillingworth. But she is a complex figure, and Hawthorne sees that her natural vigor must also lead her into further trouble. In being faithful to what he called the truth of the human heart, Hawthorne had to see that the most interesting battle was not between the heart and the intellect but within the heart itself. Hester is not properly penitent. She compounds the sin of passion with the sin of pride. She embroiders the scarlet letter as an elaborate expression of ambiguous defiance and guilt, and she dresses her daughter in equally flamboyant colors. Then, when her daughter asks her about the meaning of the letter, she lies to the child and thus underlines for us the damaging evasiveness of their relationship.

Hester's passion, then, has only been dammed up. Hawthorne has described her as the dark heroine of romantic fiction, with a "rich, voluptuous, Oriental characteristic," and the confinement of her rich, dark hair under a tight cap symbolizes the artificial restraint of her natural passion. Hawthorne sees clearly that, just as her warm generosity leads her to help Dimmesdale by proposing an escape from Boston, it also takes a humanly imperfect form. At the end of her long isolation, she leaps passionately at her last chance for freedom and happiness. Combined inextricably with her natural pity for Dimmesdale is her natural, passionate love for him and her desire for happiness. Their relationship cannot exclude passionate affection. She throws the scarlet letter aside and lets down her dark hair. "'The past is gone'" she cries, "'. . . See! With this symbol, I undo it all, and make it as [if] it had never been!'"

But of course the past cannot be undone, and little Pearl, the living result of the past—the emblem also of responsibility to the community for one's past actions—will not come to Hester until her mother puts on the familiar letter again and pins up her hair once more. Hester becomes truly, voluntarily penitent only after her lover has died; only then does she return to New England without a selfish motive.

Dimmesdale, the secret sinner, is also a remarkable study

in psychology. His private, partial penitence only becomes a greater punishment, for he shows remarkable cunning in punishing himself by vague hints of confession that work to his public benefit. Throughout the book he denies his natural, human connection with Hester and their child. His awareness of his own guilt keeps his preaching at a level that the most lowly can understand; but the more revered he becomes in his public success, the more painfully he realizes that his every public action violates his cardinal principle of honesty, or truth. The principle he violates is the most important article of Puritan belief and of nineteenth-century romantic individualism: the requirement that a man be a *true* believer, or a *true* confessor, that he reveal to God and to the world what he really is.

Thus it is a mistake to believe that with Dimmesdale, any more than with Hester, Hawthorne concentrates only on the original sin of adultery. Both morally and psychologically, Dimmesdale re-enacts a graver, far more damaging fault every day. His worst punishment is that *all other reality becomes unreal.* Knowing that his penitence is false but unable to think long about other things, he extends his egotism outward into the universe, interpreting a comet and other phenomena as messages sent directly from God to himself. His agony is so severe that the letter "A" which he has secretly seared into his flesh is not too extreme a symbol of his self-torture. His self-punishment is psychological as well as physical. . . .

CHILLINGWORTH, "THE UNPARDONABLE SINNER"

Roger Chillingworth represents Hawthorne's idea of the unpardonable sinner. Hawthorne, fascinated by the problem of guilt and forgiveness, had once asked in his notebooks what might constitute the unpardonable sin; his answer had come in language that was appropriate to Christian and romantic terminology: the violation of another soul, another heart, simply for the purpose of finding out how it would react. Chillingworth is almost wholly intellectual. From the beginning, he voluntarily isolates himself. Having married a passionate woman much younger than himself, he has sent her alone to the New World; when he discovers her disgrace, he denies his very identity—presumably in order to avoid being known for a cuckold, but also to seek revenge. He thus abandons almost all his human claims on society. He resolves to pursue the secret, *"if only for the art's sake."* With cold science, and a hint of black arts learned from savages in the wilderness, he pries into Dimmesdale's heart for the secret, and he seeks an absolutely perfect revenge: he wants to appear as the best friend to his worst enemy, so that he may torture at will and at last destroy Dimmesdale's soul. His desperate effort in the last scene to prevent Dimmesdale from confessing on the scaffold thus has its allegorical and its psychological validity. Chillingworth's very existence depends on Dimmesdale; curiosity and revenge constitute the obsession that has consumed his life.

Always, then, along with the allegory and the fundamental moral emphasis, Hawthorne is faithful to human psychology, and it is the fusion of these two that gives the book much of its value. In blending them Hawthorne reveals magnificent control of point of view, the position from which the action is seen, for he presents the most important interpretations of individual objects and actions as the interpretations of seventeenth-century characters. Let us consider two kinds of examples, the one a character and the other a series of physical phenomena.

PEARL'S ROLE

Consider first the wildness of little Pearl, the child of the two guilty lovers. To her mother and to all the Puritan characters she is a living emblem of the mother's sin; a major part of Hawthorne's criticism of Puritan thinking is that society's insistence on seeing human beings merely as emblems. In the action of the novel, moreover, Pearl represents the conscience of the community, and evidence that the community is inevitably concerned in the actions of individuals who may wish to escape it. But we must notice that Hawthorne calls little Pearl "a born outcast of the infantile world." He portrays her as an anxious child, what today we would call a hostile child. He takes great care to show us from the opening scene of the book that the infant's mother communicates her own turmoil to the child. With remarkable skill he presents this sort of evidence through the mother's eyes and through the Puritan community's interpretation. The infant, clutched tightly by the mother during the ordeal on the scaffold, "reflects the warfare of Hester's spirit" by breaking into convulsions. Both the mother and other people in the community expect the child to show signs of her sinful origin, and so *they* interpret Pearl's violent temper and some of her wisely perceptive questions as evidence of her bondage to the Devil. What Hawthorne shows us through their interpretations, then, are the natural consequences of a childhood in which the community rejects mother and child, in which an anxious, confused, rebellious mother persists in asking, "Child, what art thou?" and then allows the child to be ruled, not by discipline, but by impulse.

Hawthorne amasses this evidence so skillfully that careless readers are apt to be deceived by the allegorical interpretations into thinking the child preternaturally gifted. What we must remember is that almost every interpretation of Pearl's behavior comes to us through the mind of some seventeenth-century observer and that the child herself has every reason to ask the penetrating questions she asks: Why does her mother wear a scarlet letter? Why does the pale minister who argued so eloquently before the Governor for Hester Prynne's right to retain custody of the child hold the child's hand on the scaffold at midnight, but not in broad daylight? Why does her mother take off the letter and the tight cap in the wild forest, where no child could fail to notice that a new intimacy seems to exist with the minister?

SYMBOLS EXPAND THE MEANING

Hawthorne's introduction of symbols is also doubly effective, for he takes excellent advantage of the Puritans' habit of interpreting the smallest signs as expressions of the will of God. The real Puritans actually interpreted an event such as the killing of a snake in a church as a sign from the divine Providence that governed all human affairs, and Hawthorne had read Puritan journals in which extraordinary phenomena such as the appearance of a comet and more ordinary events such as a mouse's chewing pages from the Book of Common Prayer were seriously interpreted as providential warnings. Throughout *The Scarlet Letter* Hawthorne shows us such phenomena and the Puritan characters' reading of them. One of the most memorably effective is the suit of armor that Pearl and Hester encounter in the hall of the Governor's mansion when Hester comes there to plead for her right to retain the child. In the convex breastplate Pearl sees that the scarlet letter on her mother's breast is reflected in a monstrously magnified form and that the woman herself is almost dwarfed behind it. Through the mother's reaction to this image Hawthorne lets us see (without commenting explicitly himself) how monstrously the society had magnified the importance of one person's sin, and of all sin, so that the individual character and the individual soul and perhaps the individual sin were virtually hidden from view.

AMBIGUITY INTENSIFIES THE MYSTERY

The same kind of double relevance gives great value to Hawthorne's exploitation of the natural landscape in this novel. For the seventeenth-century Puritans the city of Boston and the colony of Massachusetts Bay represented the orderly outpost of God's people in the hostile world of the godless, and for them the American wilderness was the realm of disorder, the last stronghold of the Devil. In the romantic world of nineteenth-century American thought, the domain of untouched nature was not far different from this demonic wilderness, for there one's most primitive feelings, the individual will, ungoverned by any notion of divine authority or universal ethics, might find free expression. The wilderness in which Hester Prynne meets Arthur Dimmesdale is thus a bewilderingly ambiguous territory. As we smile at the Puritan's rudimentary effort to read the meaning of natural signs, Hawthorne does not let us forget that the meaning of external nature, like the facts and meaning of human history and the world of human psychology, remains a mystery. Is the forest the domain of evil or the domain of natural love? Does the settlement of the American wilderness bring order and godliness and progress or injustice and misery and crime?

The riddle extends, as I have suggested, to human history itself, not merely to the meaning but even to the facts. In this novel the market place of the new city of Boston is dominated by the gloomy prison, which already seems black with age, and by the scaffold; it is the scaffold that dominates Hawthorne's novel. Yet in spite of all that the narrator can do to reconstruct from a few musty records the life, the unforgettable feelings, of such characters as Hester Prynne, he cannot know and he cannot tell us some of the most important facts. At the end of the novel, Hawthorne is careful to point out, the historian must recognize a certain confusion about what the Reverend Mr. Dimmesdale had done before he died on the scaffold. As we read the dramatic scene itself we have no doubt that Dimmesdale confesses as he embraces Hester and Pearl. But later the honest narrator must tell us that "highly respectable witnesses" denied that the minister had revealed an "A" seared into the flesh over his heart; indeed, they denied that Dimmesdale had ever confessed or even "remotely implied" his complicity in the guilt of Hester Prynne.

THE ENDING ASKS MORE QUESTIONS

I do not believe that Hawthorne means to throw the entire story into confusion at this point. What he does is to remind us that our knowledge of men and their actions is as limited as our knowledge of the meaning of natural phenomena. The little we can be certain of is symbolized by the scraps of evidence that remain, and among them one of the most certain, one of the most universal, is the device on Hester Prynne's tombstone: on a black field, the red letter "A." Just as the characters in the novel interpret phenomena according to their preconceptions, so we may interpret this last symbol in the book according to our own lights. Yet we cannot fail to consider the possibility that this final device might represent two certainties of human fate: the luridness of sin and the blackness of death. The futility of human effort, in the dead certainty of oblivion and the virtual impossibility of knowing truly, hangs like a pall over this magnificently gloomy book.

Hawthorne brought to the American novel an admirable talent for symbolism and a serious interest in historical fidelity, psychological truth, and social order. No English or American novelist before him had been able to represent so convincingly the feelings and thoughts of a passionate woman, and scarcely any American novelist had posed such forcefully critical questions for prevailing nineteenth-century beliefs. It is easy to understand, therefore, why Herman Melville greeted Hawthorne's work with the shock of recognition. In the combination of allegory and historical romance Hawthorne required citizens of the land or progress to consider fundamental questions about human ability and human history. His best book continues to pose these questions for us more than a century later.

CHAPTER 2

Characters in *The Scarlet Letter*

READINGS ON
THE SCARLET LETTER

Characters in
The Scarlet Letter

Edward Wagenknecht

Edward Wagenknecht, professor of English at Boston
University, launches into a detailed analysis of the
main characters in *The Scarlet Letter*. Wagenknecht
also includes the opinions of other literary critics.

Hawthorne began work on *The Scarlet Letter* in September
1849 and finished it on February 3, 1850, while one end was
in the press in Boston and the other still in his head in
Salem. During its production he had been enough absorbed
in it to remain at his desk sometimes for nine hours a day,
but though he realized that some portions were "powerfully
written," he was sufficiently convinced that it was too dismal in tone to be successful on its own so that for a time he
planned to publish it in a collection of "Old-Time Legends"
in which it should occupy only half the total space. Even
after it had succeeded, he sometimes tried to persuade himself that it owed its popularity to the long introductory sketch
of "The Custom House," so hopelessly out of tune with the
story itself. This introduction does relate (nonfactually) how
the narrator found the scarlet letter and reference to Hester
Prynne in the Custom House ("there seemed to be here the
groundwork of a tale"), and it is true that Hawthorne's own
recent dismissal from the customs service and what he
wrote about his former associates there did for a time give
the book a topical, even slightly scandalous, interest it would
not otherwise have had. . . .

James T. Fields published the book on March 15, 1850,
bravely venturing a first printing of 2,500 copies and . . . he
was more than justified by a sale of six thousand copies during six months. When the child Henry James saw a copy in
his parents' house, he wondered what kind of a letter it
might be that was written on red paper. Grown up, he

Excerpted from *Nathaniel Hawthorne: The Man, His Tales and Romances* by Edward
Wagenknecht. Copyright 1989 by Edward Wagenknecht. Reprinted with the permission of The Continuum Publishing Company.

judged the novel to possess "that charm, very hard to express, which we find in an artist's work, the first time he has touched his highest mark—a sort of straightness and naturalness of execution, an unconsciousness of his public, and freshness of interest in his theme." Hawthorne received a royalty of fifteen percent, but since the list price was only seventy-five cents, *The Scarlet Letter* earned him only $1,500 during his lifetime.

A BOOK OF "STRAIGHTFORWARD SIMPLICITY"

It may seem odd, on first consideration, that such gigantic critical commentary should have been inspired by a story of such classical, straightforward simplicity. To all intents and purposes, there are only four characters: the Reverend Arthur Dimmesdale; Hester Prynne, who has committed adultery with him before the book begins; their daughter Pearl; and the husband, Roger Prynne, alias Chillingworth, who, upon his arrival, dedicates his life to ferreting out the minister's secret. The time scheme embraces seven years, beginning in 1642, but there is very little action, and what there is is presented mainly in a series of tableaux, with the three scaffold scenes standing at the beginning, the middle, and the end. In the first, Hester stands alone, exposed before the multitude, with her baby in her arms. In the second, Dimmesdale, tormented by his conscience, mounts the scaffold under the cloak of night, in a kind of histrionic anticipation of his genuine confession and self-exposure at the end. In the last, he finally solves his problem by his repentance and death. "I should think it might possibly succeed as an opera," Hawthorne himself remarked, "though it would certainly fail as a play."

The tableaux are linked by what Edith Wharton would have called "orchestral" passages—that is, chapters of straight narrative, each covering a particular phase or period, some of which run into brief passages of dialogue toward the end. In general the dialogue is formal and dignified, keeping at its best the calm, cool distance of art, but sometimes, especially with Pearl, lapsing into artificiality. The author is always outside his narrative ("it was a circumstance to be noted, on the morning when our story opens"). He frequently reminds us that his action is set in the past ("the new abode of the two friends . . . was in a house covering pretty nearly the site on which the venerable struc-

ture of King's Chapel has since been built"). Nor does he
ever shrink from authorial comment upon his narrative or
attempt to conceal his own value judgments. . . . For the au-
thenticity he achieves, Hawthorne depends upon his own intimate knowledge and understanding of the Puritan world
and mind and not upon either physical furnishings or ar-
chaic language. . . .

PRIDE OUT OF PUNISHMENT

The scarlet A *that Hester is sentenced to wear is intended
as a punishment, a mark of her disgrace. Hester complies
with the sentence, but not with its intent. Instead, she defiantly
embroiders a beautiful red* A, *which onlookers view with admiration. As Hawthorne points out in* The Scarlet Letter, *some of
the village gossips immediately recognized her act as a form of
disobedience.*

"She hath good skill at her needle, that's certain," remarked
one of the female spectators; "but did ever a woman, before
this brazen hussy, contrive such a way of showing it! Why,
gossips, what is it but to laugh in the faces of our godly magistrates, and make a pride out of what they, worthy gentlemen,
meant for a punishment?"

"It were well," muttered the most iron-visaged of the old
dames, "if we stripped Madam Hester's rich gown off her
dainty shoulders; and as for the red letter, which she hath
stitched so curiously, I'll bestow a rag of mine own rheumatic
flannel, to make a fitter one!"

"O, peace, neighbours, peace!" whispered their youngest
companion. "Do not let her hear you! Not a stitch in that embroidered letter, but she has felt it in her heart."

In the opening "scene," the women standing about the pillory serve as a kind of "chorus," expressing the outraged
sense of the community and especially the female portion
thereof. . . . One young matron and a man are more sympathetic however, and the author skillfully manages the scene
so as to cause the reader to agree with them. "There can be
no outrage, methinks, against our common nature . . . more
flagrant than to forbid the culprit to hide his face for shame."
He even dares to suggest that "had there been a Papist
among the crowd," he might have seen in Hester and her
child a suggestion of "the image of Divine Maternity," but he
is careful not to permit the reader to suppose that his sym-

pathy with the culprit implies condoning what she has done. "Here, there was the taint of deepest sin in the most sacred quality of human life, working such effect, that the world was only the darker for this woman's beauty, and the more lost for the infant that she had borne."

Chillingworth makes his first appearance, unidentified, as a spectator of his wife's disgrace; then Dimmesdale appears, as secondary to the older clergyman, John Wilson, who bids him exhort Hester to reveal the name of her partner in sin. Dimmesdale is described before he speaks, and the description, like his exhortation, strikes his keynote. "Take heed how thou deniest to him—who, perchance, hath not the courage to grasp it for himself—the bitter, but wholesome, cup that is now presented to thy lips!" There follows, in chapter 4, the interview between Hester and Chillingworth, when he is called upon to attend her as a physician, and she accedes to his request not to reveal their relationship. The four principals are not brought together again until chapter 8, when Dimmesdale aids Hester by blocking consideration of the plan the magistrates are pondering to remove Pearl from her mother's care. . . .

SYMBOLS AND SUPERSTITIONS

I must not leave the impression, however, that the classical simplicity of *The Scarlet Letter* is unmodified by other characteristics. Both the characters and the action are soaked in symbolism, and while there is no out-and-out supernaturalism, the superstitions of the characters and of the world they inhabit hover over the narrative and, despite the author's own rationalism, enlarge the stage upon which the action is played out. Hester tells the witch lady, Mistress Hibbins, that she would have gone to the forest and signed her name in the Black Man's book had the authorities taken Pearl away from her, while the townspeople feel that Chillingworth's skill is dependent upon necromancy. In some sense all this is at least figuratively if not literally true. C.C. Walcutt has acutely observed that Hawthorne's symbols sometimes "convey different meanings from those communicated by his statements."

AMBIGUITIES

Hawthorne's characteristic ambiguity is omnipresent also. Was the light in the sky during the second scaffold scene really an *A* for *adultery*, as it seemed to Dimmesdale; or did it stand for *Angel* because the saintly John Winthrop had been translated [died] that night; or was there no such manifestation at all? When, at the end, Dimmesdale bares the hidden mark upon his bosom ("Stand any here that question God's judgment on a sinner? Behold! behold a dreadful witness of it!"), we are never told *what* was revealed. Indeed some spectators insisted there was nothing to see. The ultimate extension of this method is achieved when a few scenes are presented as real, only to have the author cast doubt upon their actuality by reducing them to a possible "parable." Thus Mistress Hibbins is only "said to have been passing by" at a crucial moment in Dimmesdale's pilgrimage, and "the tale has surely lapsed into the improbable" in recording that a wolf came to Pearl to be petted in the forest. . . .

When all is said and done however, perhaps the basic ambiguity lies in Hawthorne's presentation of his three leading characters. Hester lives—or accepts—a saintly life of service and penitence, but it is rather more than doubtful that she really repents until her return from England to Boston in the last chapter. In the great forest scene she even proposes to return to her sin and would have done so if both Dimmesdale and Chillingworth had not prevented her. The minister inflicts penitential torments upon himself without finding peace—Hawthorne calls him a "subtle but remorseful hypocrite"—yet though the strain under which he lives is clearly killing him, it also increases his effectiveness as preacher and pastor. In the pulpit the "tongue of flame" descends upon him, and his own spiritual agonies vastly increase his ability to understand and to deal with the individual sins and sufferings of his parishioners. Yet even at the end, when he heroically throws off the hypocrisy, pride, and fear that had so long made his life a living lie and mounts the steps of the scaffold at midday, he is also in a sense making a great surrender. Be the consequences what they may, he is dropping a burden he no longer has the strength to carry. But perhaps Chillingworth's position is the most paradoxical of all. As the betrayed husband, the injured party, he claims our sympathy. Yet through dedicating his life to revenge, he becomes the worst sinner of all. . . .

POSSIBLE ENGLISH SOURCES

A number of possible English sources have been suggested, mainly in connection with matters of detail. [Edmund]

Spenser's Wood of Error seems an obvious candidate for the forest scenes, and Robert Stanton has pointed out allusions to [John] Bunyan. Probably enough has been said about Hawthorne's familiarity with the Gothic novels so that I need only note here that Max L. Autrey has nominated a Victorian "blood," *Varney the Vampire,* in connection with Chillingworth. J. Jeffrey Maybrook has studied Hawthorne's use of heraldic devices, and Donald Darnell would make *The Scarlet Letter* an emblem book. Two different articles have pointed to Andrew Marvell's poem "The Unfortunate Lover" as the source of the epitaph in King's Chapel burying ground. . . .

Unquestionably however the most important sources are American. Hawthorne's inbred knowledge of New England Puritanism was more important here than any specific source, but mention may be made of Cotton Mather [Puritan minister], whose fastings may have suggested Dimmesdale's; of Governor Winthrop's *Journal,* not published complete until 1825; of Caleb Snow's *History of Boston;* and of Joseph Felt's *Annals of Salem.* One scholar has suggested [James Kirke] Paulding's "The Dumb Girl" as a conjectural source, and another has invoked Margaret Fuller as an influence upon Hester, though Ann Hutchinson, of whom Hawthorne himself speaks, seems a much better guess.

Hawthorne also drew freely upon his own earlier writings. First, there are a number of interesting journal entries: "insincerity in a man's own heart makes all his enjoyments, all that concerns him, unreal; so that his whole life must seem like a merely dramatic representation"; "a man who does penance in what might appear to onlookers the most glorious and triumphal circumstance of his life"; "a story of the effects of revenge, diabolizing him who indulges in it"; "the life of a woman, who, by the old colony law, was condemned to wear the letter A, sewed on her garment, in token of having committed adultery."

There are also passages in *The Scarlet Letter* that recall such tales as "Egotism; or The Bosom Serpent," "Ethan Brand," "The Minister's Black Veil," "The Hollow of the Three Hills," "Roger Malvin's Burial," and "Young Goodman Brown." And in "Endicott and the Red Cross" we read:

> There was likewise a young woman, with no mean share of beauty, whose doom it was to wear the letter A on the breast of her gown, in the eyes of all the world and her own children. And even her own children knew what the initial signi-

fied. Sporting with her infamy, the lost and desperate creature had embroidered the fatal token in scarlet cloth, with
golden thread and the nicest art of needlework; so that the
capital A might have been thought to mean Admirable, or
anything other than Adulteress.

But though this is the most striking passage, it is by no
means the earliest source. Probably the real origin of the
final scaffold scene lies in Hawthorne's early interest in Dr.
Johnson's penance in Uttoxeter marketplace, of which he
makes much in his "Biographical Sketches," and if "The Battle Omen" is his, he had conceived the idea of Dimmesdale's
celestial terrors as early as 1825.

Hester

It is time to turn to the direct consideration of Hawthorne's
characters. Hester Prynne, dark, beautiful of form and feature, and unmistakably of genteel background, was the first
great female character in American fiction, and though
Henry James was right in maintaining that Dimmesdale is
the principal character, in the sense that the book is built
around him and he precipitates the denouement, few readers have been as much interested in him as in her. Even
Chillingworth apprehends her stature: "I pity thee for the
good that has been wasted in thy nature."

Because Hawthorne did not believe that law can deal with
sin as distinct from crime, he makes a whole paragraph of
the sentence: "The scarlet letter had not done its office." He
seems to have felt that in placing it upon Hester's breast, the
magistrates had blasphemously usurped the function of
God, as Chillingworth later usurps it in his plot against
Dimmesdale. Yet it serves her well in freeing her from all
danger of trying to live such a lie as consumes her lover. She
presents what she is to the world at all times, so that there is
nothing left to fester inwardly.

Hester Helps the Townspeople

She conducts herself with what "might be pride" but looked
much more like humility. Her way of life suggests that she
had determined so to bear her earthly punishment without
complaint, in the place where she had incurred her guilt,
that "the torture of her daily shame would at length purge
her soul, and work out another purity than that which she
had lost." She gives so freely of her little means in charity

and of the "wellspring of human kindness" in her "warm and rich nature" in loving service and counsel that Michael Gilmore is even tempted to associate her with Catholics and Arminians as mistaking "the covenant of law for the covenant of grace" and seeking "to expiate . . . sin through good works." There were "none so self-devoted as Hester, when pestilence stalked through the town." She sensed in herself the power to detect secret sin and felt a sense of fellowship with all sinners, and she refrained from praying for her enemies only because she feared that a blessing from such as she was might turn to a curse, yet she "struggled to believe that no fellow mortal was guilty like herself." But "her breast, with its badge of shame, was but the softer pillow for the head that needed one," and as time passed, "many people refused to interpret the scarlet A by its original signification. They said it meant Able; so strong was Hester Prynne, with a woman's strength." It even came to take on "the effect of the cross on a nun's bosom. It imparted to the wearer a kind of sacredness, which enabled her to walk securely amid all peril."

All in all, Hester Prynne seems at once to share the community's judgment upon her, yet to accept herself with her past and her destiny intact. As time passes, we are told, her life "turned, in a great measure, from passion and feeling, to thought," and "she assumed a freedom of speculation, then common enough on the other side of the Atlantic, but which our forefathers. . . would have held to be a deadlier crime than that stigmatized by the scarlet letter." Had she thought herself worthy, she might have become a prophetess and "come down to us in history, hand in hand with Ann Hutchinson." Her heresies are specified, however, only to the extent that, in the last chapter, we are told that, during her later years, she looked forward to a time when "the whole relation between man and woman" should be established "on a surer ground of mutual happiness."

Except for her thoughts, which she keeps to herself, the only outlet Hester has for her creativity through her seven years' penance is the fantastic embroidery she bestows upon the very badge of her shame, the scarlet letter itself, and only such sympathetic insight as that of the young matron in the opening chapter can perceive that "not a stitch" in that article "but she has felt it in her heart." Through it she "exhibits her guilt," says John E. Hart, "yet relieves it through art and creativity." And Richard H. Brodhead adds that though "she accepts the designation of adulteress," she accepts it "on her own terms," turning it "into a more complex symbol, one that does justice to the inseparable conjunction of something guilty and something vital and fertile in her passionate nature."

HESTER AND DIMMESDALE MEET

We come then at last to the great forest scene, in which she prepares deliberately to break the chain that binds her and commit herself to open rebellion with her lover. It is quite true, as has been pointed out again and again, that the adultery of Hester and Dimmesdale was a sin of passion and impulse and that their decision to renew their guilty relationship and go away together is the much more serious sin of deliberate will and choice. Yet few critics have done full justice to Hester at this point. She does not decide until it has been made clear to her both that if Dimmesdale stays in Boston, tormented by Chillingworth and his own conscience, he will die, and that she alone can save him. "Think for me, Hester! Thou art strong! Resolve for me what to do." Both parties being what they were, this left her no choice but to decide "that he had a right to her utmost aid." It was no longer a question of what they *ought* to do, much less of what they ought to *have done* but only of what they now *could* do. There are no morals in the grave. The all-important thing now is to save Dimmesdale while there is still something left to be saved. Hester simply enacts woman's historic role of choosing the "best possible" in a very imperfect world and of cleaning up the messes men have made while she disregards all the theoretical formulations that mean too much to them. Taking another child on her hands, she sins in pure charity, but it is only fair to add that she would no more have acted thus if she had not "still so passionately [have] loved" Dimmesdale. . . . Many readers no doubt feel that Dimmesdale was not worth such devotion, but who is? and what has that to do with the case? . . .

IS DIMMESDALE A HYPOCRITE?

The difference between Hester and Dimmesdale is not only one of sex or temperament however, nor even merely that she has acknowledged her sin while his is concealed. He knows the Puritan theology as she does not know it and has a far firmer grasp upon the Puritan faith, but she lives much closer to the vital currents of life. Yet the fact that the scarlet letter has given her a "passport" into regions where he cannot follow is very important. He can violate his code under the influence of passion, but spiritually and intellectually he cannot break out of its confines. Without the stamina to be a sinner and go on living with himself, he can endure horrible mental and physical torture, but the best he can achieve by such means is to combine "the agony of heaven-defying guilt and vain repentance."

He is generally called a hypocrite, but though the life he lives is a lie, he is never quite that. Pride and fear combine to keep him from making a clean breast of things, and the best in him conspires with the worst to keep him silent. A self-called "polluted priest," he is still a faithful pastor, and he cannot bring himself to disillusion those who believe in him and to whom his ministry, besides being vastly more humane than that of most of his associates, and even more effective because of the anguish consequent upon his sin, has been—make no mistake about it—nearly ideal.

Generally speaking, Dimmesdale has met with considerably less charity from the critics than Hester. One, Edward H. Davidson, has presumed to speak not only for Hawthorne but for God in damning the minister not only in time but for eternity. Opposing those who, without arguing the case, have assumed that Hester was the seducer, Neil B. Houston argues that Dimmesdale seduced her. William B. Dillingham calls even his final confession ironical, since "he dies believing it to be a completely open and free admission, while it is hardly more specific than his earlier attempts." But it is William B. Nolte who pulls out all the stops, insisting even that Dimmesdale's confession "cost him absolutely nothing," an interpretation that obliges Nolte to conclude that "the final thirty pages . . . are certainly the weakest artistically in the novel" and that "the final scene on the scaffold lacks proper motivation." It is astonishing that a character of fiction should be able to inspire such antagonism.

In the forest scene Dimmesdale throws his burden upon Hester, and she courageously picks it up, but as Robert Stanton has observed, she can only offer him "a philosophy modelled after her temperament," and in so doing she proves that she does not really understand him. Hester is far from being a wanton, but she is no legalist either, and by casting

her out the community has made a heretic of her. Had she
and her lover fled from Boston, her painfully developed philosophy, however it be judged, might well have supplied an
adequate foundation for reasonable happiness, at least in
this life, but Dimmesdale could never have escaped, for he
would have carried Boston and the whole paraphernalia of
Boston Calvinism away with him in his heart, wherever he
might have gone.

DIMMESDALE DECIDES TO CONFESS

The immediate result of the interview in the forest however
is not only exhilarating but euphoric. Dimmesdale rushes
home to write the Election Sermon that is to crown his ministerial career in such a burst of energy as he had not known
since he became a sinner. He eats voraciously and writes furiously, expending his mental and physical energies as reck-
lessly as if he were never to need them again, which, as it
turns out, he did not. We are handicapped in our complete
understanding of what happened by the fact that we do not
hear the sermon; all we know is that Dimmesdale forecast a
glorious future for his country. Even Hester does not hear it;
all that reaches her as she stands listening in the market-
place, is the "indistinct, but varied, murmur and flow of the
minister's very peculiar voice." Neither do we know how it
differed from the other sermon, already partly written, that
he threw away, nor at what point Dimmesdale's euphoria
collapsed, and, quite without knowing that Chillingworth
had discovered his plans, he impulsively decided at last to
mount the steps of the scaffold and summon Hester and
Pearl to join him there. Perhaps it was his own rapturously
received sermon that opened up the way for God's grace to
reach out and save him at the last, which, as Darrel Abel has
convincingly shown, according to Puritan theology, it did.

The one thing we can be sure of is that the energy that
had impelled him thus far, even when he felt himself most
inspired, was basically sexual in character. He had never
been so close to damnation as in the wild temptations that
beset him on the way home to whisper blasphemies and ob-
scenities to such members of his congregation as he
chanced to encounter. He had always possessed what politi-
cians now call "charisma" and what the flesh merchants de-
nominate "sex appeal." "The virgins of his church grew pale
around him," writes Hawthorne, "victims of a passion so im-

bued with religious sentiment that they imagined it to be all religion, and brought it openly, in their white bosoms, as their most acceptable sacrifice before the altar." But never until now, except upon one occasion, had what he at least regarded as his unredeemed lower nature threatened to break through its controls.

It is the hallmark of the greatness of *The Scarlet Letter* as a work of art that its power no more depends upon the reader's faith in Calvinistic theology than Homer's power stands or falls with faith in the Greek gods. Whether he was the unhappy victim of a delusion or whether his action was prompted by a true insight into what God required of him, it still remains true that, being what he was and believing what he believed, so far as salvation in any sense of the word was still possible for Arthur Dimmesdale, he could have achieved it only by doing exactly what he did in the third and last scaffold scene.

PEARL

Pearl, Hester's daughter by Dimmesdale, comes closer to being an allegorical figure than anybody else in *The Scarlet Letter*, yet paradoxically she seems to be the only one that was studied from an actual human being—the author's own strange and exquisite daughter, Una. It may be however that, in the state of knowledge concerning prenatal influences that prevailed in his time, Hawthorne may well have thought Pearl more realistic than she is. And even so there are touches in her portrayal that are startlingly real. The book is nowhere richer in symbolism than in the forest scene, yet Pearl's impassioned reactions to the change in her mother's appearance when she unbinds her hair and discards the scarlet letter are equally true literally and symbolically. As John A. Andola remarks, "Without her mother's sin, Pearl could not exist, nor could she exist without her mother's love, both of which are symbolized in the scarlet A and in Pearl herself." But anyone who has had any experience with small children will also understand how they can react to unexpected changes in persons and things that are dear to them.

Hester named her daughter after the "pearl of great price" in the New Testament, "purchased with all she had,—her mother's only treasure." Because she dressed her, in sharp contrast to her own drab attire, in "the richest tissues that could be procured," arranged with "a fantastic ingenuity" that underlined the little girl's "fairy charm," she was in one aspect the scarlet letter come to life, and when the Reverend Mr. Wilson saw her, he thought she might better have been named "Coral" or "Ruby." She is a natural child not only because she is a bastard but because she is out of tune with society but in harmony with the forest and all the wild things in it, as they with her. "There was fire in her and throughout her; she seemed the unpremeditated offshoot of a passionate action." There seemed to be both depth and variety in her nature, but she "could not be made amenable to rules. In giving her existence, a great law had been broken, and the result was a being whose elements were perhaps beautiful and brilliant, but all in disorder." The "warfare of Hester's spirit" at the time of her conception lived again in her child. "She is my happiness," her mother says of her. "She is my torture.". . .

One must say that those who see Pearl as a holy child can make a very strong case at least so far as her relations with her parents are concerned. We have Hester's own specific though figurative word that it was Pearl alone who saved her from going to the forest and writing her name in the Black Man's book. As for Dimmesdale, when he defends her mother in chapter 8, Pearl astonishes Hester by stealing "softly towards him, and taking his hand in the grasp of both her own [and laying] her cheek against it," but she is displeased with him in the second scaffold scene because he will not promise to stand there together with her and her mother tomorrow noontide, and she refuses to kiss him in the forest scene because he is not "true." It is only in the third and final scaffold scene that she achieves full humanity, "and as her tears fell openly upon her father's cheek, they were the pledge that she would grow up amid human joy and sorrow, nor forever do battle with the world but be a woman in it." She had at last succeeded in her search for a father and thus established herself in a normal relationship to society, and here at least she justifies Anne Marie McNamara's claim that "she is grace, the instrument of [Dimmesdale's] redemption."

But if Pearl is a holy child, she is also, whether quite consistently or not, something besides, and the hypothetical inconsistency is part of her charm, for it saves her from fading away altogether into an allegory. There is "a circle of radiance" about her, and in the forest scene it is she alone whom the sunshine always follows. It is true, as Malcolm Cowley says, that "the forest is the meeting place of those who follow their passions and revolt against the community," but it is more than that, for the beasts who dwell there are without sin, and Pearl says rightly, "I wear nothing on my bosom yet." If she is inconsistent, so is nature, or at least man sees her thus. . . .

CHILLINGWORTH

The wronged husband, who calls himself Roger Chillingworth, has drawn considerably less comment than the others, and this is not surprising, for, as has already been noted, Hawthorne's villains rarely awaken his deepest powers. Chillingworth's is certainly a much better characterization than Butler's in *Fanshawe,* but essentially he is humanized only by his own free admission that he wronged Hester before she wronged him by knowingly marrying a young woman who did not love him and, more doubtfully, by his not quite convincing bequest of his property to Pearl, whose becoming "the richest heiress of her day in the New World" is the one point where *The Scarlet Letter* skirts the sensational story papers.

Originally "kindly, though not of warm affections, but ever, and in all his relations with the world, a pure and upright man," Chillingworth becomes guilty of what Hawthorne saw as the unpardonable sin by probing Dimmesdale's heart without sympathy, under the guise of ministering to him as a physician, until he has come close to murdering him, both physically and spiritually. Even that champion self-tormentor is able to realize at last that "that old man's revenge has been blacker than my sin. He has violated, in cold blood, the sanctity of a human heart."

Chillingworth's realization of his own large and initial share in the tragedy that has overtaken all three persons is weakened and robbed of its cleansing power by his conviction that everything that has occurred is the result of a "dark necessity." "My old faith, long forgotten," he says, "comes back to me, and explains all that we do, and all we suffer." He is indeed a perverted Calvinist, and . . . his story is developed in the full light of Christian and Puritan theological beliefs. It was in connection with *The Scarlet Letter* that Theodore T. Munger made his pregnant statement that "whatever a man does, he does to himself," and it is therefore not surprising that as time passes, Chillingworth should grow "duskier" and "more misshapen" until at last he has become virtually a fiend (at this point surely he is as much an allegorical figure as Pearl ever becomes). . . . The author's insight was sound . . . when he killed him off within a year of Dimmesdale's death. What was there left for him to live for? And what could have been more suitable than that he should have "almost vanished from mortal sight like an up-rooted weed that lies wilting in the sun"? It may be that evil is negative, not positive, being only the absence of good, but falling in hate can be as overwhelming an experience as falling in love; it is fortunate that it occurs much more rarely.

"What we did had a consecration of its own," Hester tells Dimmesdale in the forest, but it is clear enough that though Hawthorne viewed what had happened with complete sympathy and understanding, he did not agree with her. Surely Dante [Alighieri, the Italian poet] himself might have been satisfied with Hawthorne's considered pronouncement in chapter 18: "And be the stern and sad truth spoken, that the breach which guilt has made into the human soul is never, in this mortal state, repaired." Even in her final phase, living a virtually saintly life, Hester "had long since recognized the impossibility that any mission of divine and mysterious truth should be confided to a woman stained with sin, bowed down with shame, or even burdened with a lifelong sorrow."

Yet while this is what *The Scarlet Letter* "means," it also means more than this or any other formulation; otherwise it would not be a work of art but a sermon; we could stop with the formulation and dispense with the art altogether. . . .

Interpretations of works of art are necessary, but no critic can formulate more than he has been able to perceive, and *The Scarlet Letter* is greater than any interpretation of it. That is why it has outlived so many and may be trusted to outlive so many more.

The Characters Reveal the Story's Meaning

Hyatt H. Waggoner

Hyatt H. Waggoner, professor of American literature at Brown University, analyzes the changing moral values of Hester, Dimmesdale, and Chillingworth throughout *The Scarlet Letter*. According to Waggoner, the effects of their guilt preclude happiness for any of them; only Pearl, who has moved to another country, has a chance for a positive life.

The Scarlet Letter is the most nearly static of all Hawthorne's novels. There is very little external action. We can see one of the evidences for this, and perhaps also one of the reasons for it, when we compare the amount of space Hawthorne devotes to exposition and description with the amount he devotes to narration. It is likewise true, in a sense not yet fully explored, that on the deepest level of meaning the novel has only an ambiguous movement. But in between the surface and the depths movement is constant and complex, and it is in this middle area that the principal value of the work lies.

The movement may be conceived as being up and down the lines of natural and moral value, lines which, if they were to be represented in a diagram, should be conceived as crossing to form an *X*. Thus, most obviously, Hester's rise takes her from low on the line of moral value, a "scarlet woman" guilty of a sin black in the eyes of the Puritans, to a position not too remote from Mr. Wilson's, as she becomes a sister of mercy and the light of the sickroom: this when we measure by the yardstick of community approval. When we apply a standard of measurement less relativistic, we are also likely to find that there has been a "rise." I suppose most of us will agree, whatever our religion or philosophy may be, that Hester has gained in stature and dignity by enduring and transcending suffering, and that she has grown in

Excerpted from *Hawthorne: A Critical Study* by Hyatt H. Waggoner (Cambridge: Belknap Press, Harvard University Press, 1963). Copyright ©1955, 1963 by the President and Fellows of Harvard College. Reprinted by permission of the publisher.

awareness of social responsibility. Like all tragic protagonists, she has demonstrated the dignity and potentialities of
man, even in her defeat.

Dimmesdale is a more complicated, though less admirable and sympathetic, figure. He first descends from his
original position as the saintly guide and inspiration of the
godly to the position he occupies during the greater part of
the novel as very nearly the worst of the sinners in his
hypocrisy and cowardice, then reascends by his final act of
courageous honesty to a position somewhere in between his
reputation for light and his former reality of darkness. . . .

As he himself sees it, at any rate, he has emerged at last
not only into the light of day but into that which shines from
the celestial city. He sees Chillingworth's persecution as
Providential: he has been saved despite himself, by the very
intensity of his suffering. But we note that the words that
characterize his death as triumphant and suggest a salvation
in a life beyond death are his, not Hawthorne's. Hawthorne's
last word on the subject comes in the description of the
tombstone, in the novel's closing sentences, and there the
ambiguity is complete. . . .

As for Chillingworth, he of course descends, but not to
reascend. As in his injured pride and inhuman curiosity he
devotes himself to prying into the minister's heart, whatever
goodness had been his—which had always been negative,
the mere absence of overt evil—disappears and pride moves
into what had been a merely cold heart, prompting to revenge and displacing intellectual curiosity, which continues
only as a rationalization, a "good" reason serving to distract
attention from the real one. He becomes a moral monster
who feeds only on another's torment, divorced wholly from
the sources of life and goodness. He is eloquent testimony to
the belief that Hawthorne shared with [William] Shakespeare and [Herman] Melville, among others: that it is possible for man to make evil his good.

MORAL VALUES

Thus the three principal characters move up and down the
scale of moral values in a kind of counterpoint: Chillingworth clearly down, Hester ambiguously up, Dimmesdale in
both directions, first down, then up, to end somewhere above
the center. But this is not the end of the matter. Because there
are obscure but real relationships, if only of analogy, be-

tween the moral and the natural (I am using "natural" in the sense of those aspects of existence studied by the natural sciences, which do not include the concept of freedom of choice among their working principles or their assumptions), because there are relations between the moral and the natural, the movements of the characters up and down the scale of moral values involve them in symbolic movements on the scale of natural values. The moral journeys are, in fact, as we have abundantly seen, largely suggested by physical imagery. Chillingworth becomes blacker and more twisted as he becomes more evil. Hester's beauty withers under the scorching brand, then momentarily reasserts itself in the forest scene, then disappears again. Dimmesdale becomes paler and walks more frequently in the shadow as his torment increases and his sin is multiplied.

"LAWS AGAINST PREVAILING INIQUITIES"

As punishment for her sin, the Puritans sentenced Hester to stand on the scaffold in public view for three hours; she was also forced to wear an A, symbolizing her adultery, on the front of her dress for the rest of her life. In 1694, Salem's official law was even more severe, as this excerpt from the "Annals of Salem" records.

May 5th, 1694. * * * A memorial was received, signed by many clergymen, desiring the Legislature to enact laws against prevailing iniquities. Among such laws, passed this session, were two against Adultery and Polygamy. Those guilty of the first crime, were to sit an hour on the gallows, with ropes about their necks,—be severely whipt not above 40 stripes; and forever after wear a capital A, two inches long, cut out of cloth coloured differently from their clothes, and sewed on the arms, or back parts of their garments so as always to be seen when they were about. The other crime, stated with suitable exceptions, was punishable with death.

But the moral changes are not simply made visible by the changes in the imagery: in their turn they require the visible changes and determine their direction. The outstanding example of this is of course Chillingworth's transformation. As we infer the potential evil in him from the snake imagery, the deformity, and the darkness associated with him when we first see him, so later his dedication to evil as his good suggests the "fancy" of the lurid flame in his eyes and the "notion" that it would be appropriate if he blasted the beauty of nature wherever he walked. So too the minister's moral journey suggests to the minds of the people both the red stigma which some think they see over his heart and the red *A* in the sky, with its ambiguous significance of angel or adultery. . . .

PEARL ESCAPES PUNISHMENT

All three of the chief characters, in short, exist on both of our crossed lines, the moral and the natural. They are seen in two perspectives, not identical but obscurely related. Pearl's situation, however, is somewhat different. She seems not to exist on the moral plane at all. She is an object of natural beauty, a flower, a gem, instinctively trusted by the wild creatures of the forest. She is as incapable of deceit or dishonesty as nature itself, and at times as unsympathetic. She is not good or bad, because she is not responsible. Like the letter on her mother's breast, she is an emblem of sin. Like the red spot over the minister's heart, she is also a result of sin. But she is not herself a moral agent. Even when she torments her mother with her demands for the truth, or refuses to acknowledge the minister until he acknowledges them, she is not bad, she is merely natural. She is capricious with an animal's, or a small child's, lack of understanding of the human situation and consequent lack of responsiveness to emotions which it cannot understand. . . .

THE "DARKENING CLOSE"

Since "history" is created by the interaction of natural conditions and human choice, there is a significant sense in which Pearl has no history in the story. She moves in and out of the foreground, a bright spot of color in a gloomy scene, serving to remind Hester of her sin and the reader of the human condition by the absence of one of its two poles in her being, but never becoming herself fully human. In the final scaffold scene Hawthorne shows us Pearl weeping for the first time and tells us that her tears "were the pledge that she would grow up amid human joy and sorrow, nor forever do battle with the world, but be a woman in it." In the "Conclusion," when Hawthorne gives us a glimpse of the years following the real end of his tale in the minister's confession, he suggests that Pearl grew to happy womanhood abroad. If so, she must have taken her place with Hester and Dimmesdale and Chillingworth in the realm of moral values, making her history and being made by it.

But the others, including the Puritan populace, have histories and are involved in the larger movements of history created by all of them together existing in nature as creatures and moral beings. Hester might not have committed adultery had Chillingworth had a warmer heart, or perhaps even had he been younger or less deformed. He might not have fallen from a decent moral neutrality to positive vice had she not first fallen. Hester is forced to become stronger because the minister is so weak, and he gains strength by contact with her strength when they meet again in the forest. Chillingworth is stimulated by his victim's helplessness to greater excesses of torment and sin, and the Puritan women around the scaffold are stirred by Hester's youth and beauty to greater cruelty than was implicit in their inquisition anyway. St. Paul's "We are members one of another" could be taken as a text to be illustrated by the histories of human hearts recounted in the novel.

Yet with all this complex movement on two planes, with all this richness, this density, of history, when we ask ourselves the final questions of meaning and value we find the movement indecisive or arrested in one direction, continuing clearly only in the other. The Puritan people and Chillingworth are condemned, but are Hester and Dimmesdale redeemed? It is significant in this connection that Pearl's growth into womanhood takes place after the end of the story proper. It is also significant that though Hester bore her suffering nobly, it is not clear that she ever repented; and that, though he indulged in several kinds of penance, it is possible to doubt that the minister ever did. . . .

The "darkening close" of this "tale of human frailty and sorrow" is only slightly relieved by the conclusion, which affords us a glimpse of happiness for Pearl in another time and place. The novel's darkness is related to "history" in another sense than the one in which I have been using the word—to history as the specifically Puritan past, as Hawthorne interpreted it. Because Puritan society was as it was, and because Hester and Arthur were both, in different degrees, of it as well as in it, there could be no really happy ending for them. Personal factors in Hawthorne's life may have entered into the mood of the work, to be sure. He wrote it while grief over the death of his mother was still intense and he was depressed by his dismissal from the Custom House position. It was a dark time for him. But more relevantly from the standpoint of judging the inner integrity of the novel he produced, the darkness is demanded by the nature of the materials. When he tells us that the Puritans were a people among whom religion and law were almost identical, the implication is clear: such a combination spoiled both the religion and the law, especially when the religious legalism rested on Biblical literalism. No wonder a jail, a gallows, and a cemetery dominate the scene in the first chapter, with only a single rose bush, blooming in an unpropitious site, suggesting the reality of anything else than sin and death.

We can now see that the opening chapter contains not only the thematic material that Hawthorne will develop but, implicitly, his final judgment of the Puritans. Hawthorne is expressing a view very typical of him when he says that "the deep heart of Nature," expressing itself through the rose, the traditional symbol of love, could "pity and be kind" to the prisoner, but the Puritans could only condemn and punish.

The Role of Pearl

Anne Marie McNamara

Readers and critics alike have pondered the role of
Pearl in *The Scarlet Letter*. Critics call the child
"precocious," "thoroughly disagreeable," "a spirit,"
"an imp," "an elf." Others have even suggested that
Hawthorne should have omitted Pearl from the book.
In contrast, Anne Marie McNamara, who taught at
Catholic University and Sacred Heart College,
believes that Pearl is crucial to Hawthorne's handling
of Dimmesdale.

In discussions of Nathaniel Hawthorne's *The Scarlet Letter*,
little attention has been given to the significance of Pearl, the
illegitimate daughter of Hester Prynne and Arthur Dimmesdale. Indifference to her role in the plot is surprising in view
of the general assumption that lack of motivation for the
confession of Dimmesdale is a radical weakness in the plot.
Since it is obvious that neither Hester nor Chillingworth
constitutes an external cause for Dimmesdale's *volte face*
[about-face], it seems reasonable to consider the possibility
that Pearl may be the agent who effects his unexpected public confession of paternity. If Pearl is a part of the "electric
chain" formed as she, Dimmesdale, and Hester join hands in
the darkness and stand on the pillory as a family for the first
time, it may not be illogical to assume that she is as dynamic
a force in the plot as are the other two members of the chain.

The narrator's extensive treatment of the child, his careful
delineation of her physical and spiritual qualities, his presentation of her in juxtaposition to both Hester and Dimmesdale, and his use of her in every decisive scene seem to jus-
tify an assumption that she is more than a passive link
between her father and mother and more than a static symbol of their sin. Above all, his insistence upon the peculiar
preternatural quality of the child and his manipulation of
this phenomenon in the crucial scenes (the forest scene and

Excerpted from "The Character of Flame: The Function of Pearl in *The Scarlet Letter*"
by Anne Marie McNamara, *American Literature*, vol. 27, no. 4 (December 1956). Copyright 1956, Duke University Press. Reprinted with permission.

the three pillory scenes) must certainly indicate that she is not merely a fantastically decorative "relief" in the somber story but a functional element in the structural design. . . .

WHY DOES DIMMESDALE CHANGE?

If *The Scarlet Letter* is Dimmesdale's story, it must trace the change within him from the condition of a sinner, a hypocrite, and a weak capitulator to Hester's plea for flight and resumption of sin, to that of a penitent, sincere and strong enough (and just barely strong enough) to make public confession. But there must be a cause for the change. I suggest that it is Pearl in her "otherworldly" aspect. Since the change in Dimmesdale is in the spiritual order, the cause may be assumed to be in the same order. Pearl is a spirit-child. As such she operates plausibly as an efficient cause within the *ambiance* of ambiguity which pervades the novel. She causes a transformation in the realm of the spirit; the effect is translatable in the terms of the spirit. Above and beyond the literal reality of her action as Hester's and Dimmesdale's child, she moves authoritatively as a regenerative influence on the level of *operative* symbol. On this level, *The Scarlet Letter* is the story of an extraordinary man redeemed by the extraordinary action of an extraordinary child. The progress of such a redemption in such a realm seems to me to take place in four stages: Preparation (Chapters I–XVI); Communication (Chapters XVII–XIX); Transformation (Chapters XX–XXII); and Revelation (Chapter XXIII).

The first of these stages consists of a meticulous preparation for the cause-effect relationship between Pearl and Dimmesdale, a relationship which depends upon the capability of the one to initiate and of the other to receive the impetus to regenerative action. For such capability in Pearl and for such susceptibility in Dimmesdale the narrator through sixteen chapters most carefully and elaborately provides. By detailing and dissecting the relationship of each of the two with one of the other major characters, he reveals in both certain peculiar spiritual and psychological qualities which he will juxtapose as he brings them face to face in the crucial forest scene for their first major meeting. Before this central scene, he presents Pearl in relation to Hester, Dimmesdale in relation to Chillingworth. Gradually and cumulatively, he draws first one, then the other, carefully keeping them apart except for four brief but pregnant meetings.

DIFFERENT LEVELS OF UNDERSTANDING

In this preparation for their decisive encounter, in which the intercourse between them will be effected on a preternatural plane, he presents each of them on two distinct levels: the ordinary and the extraordinary, or the literal and the figurative, or the natural and the preternatural. Neither the child nor the man, he shows, is merely an ordinary being. Pearl is not merely an ordinary, playful seven-year-old child: she is also precociously intelligent, bewilderingly subtle, frighteningly independent, and penetratingly wise. A double-natured anomaly, torturing her mother with misgivings of her natural origin, she exhibits even in babyhood an uncanny curiosity concerning Hester's scarlet letter. From early childhood, she displays unearthly inquisitiveness about the minister's habit of placing his hand over his heart. Most significantly, by curious questioning and implication and with a prescience that can only be described as preternatural, she insistently associates these two ostensibly disparate phenomena. Similarly, Dimmesdale is not only a well-loved and devoted minister: he is a godlike figure in the community, admired for his delicate understanding and sympathy and superbly endowed with intellectual acumen and spiritual perspicuity. Above all, he is blessed almost beyond human capacity with the gift of communication. It is of the utmost importance to observe that in spite of the physical and moral deterioration resulting from his own conscience and from Chillingworth's vindictive ministrations, his profound insight, his acute perception, and his delicate spiritual sensitivity remain unimpaired.

With such preparation, the preternaturally endowed child and man are brought together by the narrator in a cause-effect relationship in the great forest scene. I suggest that the second stage in the process of Dimmesdale's redemption takes place in the three chapters which constitute this scene (Chaps. XVII, XVIII, XIX). It is the critical stage of Communication. Everything in the arrangement of details is powerfully suggestive of duality: in the setting, light and darkness, land and water; in the mood, love and disdain, desire and fear, acceptance and rejection, reconciliation and estrangement; in the atmosphere, the real and the preternatural. Against this background, the duality that has already been elaborately established in Pearl and in Dimmesdale begins to operate in a remarkably subtle context of ambiguity.

PEARL'S DUAL NATURE

The double nature of little Pearl functions in this environment on two distinct levels (the natural and the preternatural), in two directions (towards a known and an unknown parent), through two sets of actions (the explicit and the implicit) translatable upon two planes of meaning (the literal and the figurative). She approaches and affects Hester and Dimmesdale in appropriately different ways suited to the capacity of each to receive and understand her meaning. On the natural level she acts on Hester as a real child; on the preternatural level she acts on Dimmesdale as a "more-than-child," an elf-dryad-nymph, a spirit child. In each case, her method of approach is determined by the nature of the desired effect. In Hester the need is for the restoration of the discarded public acknowledgment of adultery, the embroidered scarlet letter. In Dimmesdale the desideratum is the revelation of the private, hidden stigma of the same sin. . . .

But the estrangement between Pearl and Dimmesdale is not a temporary condition, induced by one overt act and dissipated by another. The offense of her father against her is the deliberate and guilty concealment of parenthood during her whole lifetime. The healing of this serious breach (divined by the elf-nature but not by the child-nature in Pearl) cannot be effected as was the other, immediately, visibly, audibly, objectively. The spirit child communicates her disapproval in another way, one exquisitely appropriate to Dimmesdale's sensibility—through a silent, indirect, subjective language. In the entire scene at the brookside she does not speak to him with her human voice at all. She addresses him indirectly through her persistent rejection of his advances and through actions ostensibly directed towards her mother. . . .

Pearl's actions at the brookside nettle her mother and produce immediate and tangible results. They work differently on Dimmesdale. For him they have more than their superficial meaning. His fancy that the brook flowing between Pearl and her parents is a boundary between two worlds may suggest his awareness of the double level of Pearl's action. His comment is eloquent: he says that the brook separates Pearl from Hester; he does not say that it separates Pearl from him. On the other hand, when Hester is about to call to Pearl to join her and the minister, the child's distance from them is judged differently by the two. To Hester, Pearl is "not far off," but to Dimmesdale she is "a good way off."

Does he mean that she seems to be in another world from which she is reaching out to him? . . .

Although Pearl's outburst at the brookside is directed towards her mother, it affects Dimmesdale traumatically. This hypersensitive man experiences almost simultaneously the extremes of exaltation and depression—Hester's plan for the resumption of their love affair and Pearl's adamant rejection of his affection. His unacknowledged daughter tells him in her wordless language that his acquiescence to Hester's will to escape is a false answer to his problem and is distasteful to her. She will not enter into arrangements which involve a continuance of his concealment of sin. No wonder that the minister who leaves the elf at the brookside is a minister in a maze. . . .

In other references in Chapter XI, the narrator emphasizes the "preternatural activity" of Dimmesdale's intellectual and moral perceptions, his power of experiencing and communicating emotion, and his predilection for the autonomy of truth. It is obvious that the narrator has taken great care to establish Dimmesdale as a fit recipient for Pearl's cryptic message of truth.

DIMMESDALE BEGINS TO CHANGE

The three chapters which follow the communication in the forest constitute what may be called the phase or stage of Transformation in the process of Dimmesdale's redemption. In the context of ambiguity, the title of the first of these chapters, "The Minister in a Maze," may imply a double effect in the minister as he leaves Hester and Pearl. On a literal level, he is reeling with the physical excitement of plans for escape from Chillingworth and for resumption of his love affair with Hester. On the figurative level, however, he may be stunned and reeling from the spiritual blow dealt him by the elf-child, the meaning of which he as yet only imperfectly realizes. Through her act of rejection she has communicated to him the necessity for public declaration of sin as a prerequisite of forgiveness. "So great a vicissitude in his life could not at once be received as real." Now a *vicissitude* is a *change.* The term is capable of double translation: the obvious one, the projected change of his status and environment by escape to Europe; and the subtle one, the incipient interior change of his attitude towards his concealment of guilt. So strange has the experience been that it seems to him to have been a dream. Yet he knows that it was not: he sees Pearl happily dancing along at Hester's side, now that he (the intruder on one level, the hypocritical sinner on the other) has left them. The "indistinctness and duplicity of impression" which the narrator says "vexed him with a strange disquietude" may well be the conflict in his sensitive mind between the two effects of his forest interview: the possibility of freedom (evil seen as good) and the necessity of bondage (good seen as evil). The contention between the two forces for mastery over the soul of the minister is set in motion in this tremendously meaningful chapter, all of which (with the exception of the first three paragraphs) has to do with the element of *change.*

This chapter develops the motivation generated in the forest scene for the minister's confession in the final chapter. It is in perfect harmony with the ambiguous pattern of the whole. Internal change manifested only in the final chapter is suggested here in an account of the minister's strange sense of external change in familiar objects on his homeward walk. In a long passage of eight pages, "this importunately obtrusive sense of change" is developed. The woods seem wilder; in the town, familiar landmarks seem namelessly but noticeably changed; people are unaccountably but certainly different; his own church seems unreal and dreamlike. The narrator's interpretation of this passage adumbrates the ultimate use to which he will put this provocative material: "This phenomenon in the various shapes which it assumed, *indicated no external change,* but so sudden and important a *change in the spectator* of the familiar scene, that the intervening space of a single day had operated on his consciousness like the lapse of years." The significance of this comment cannot be overestimated. It states and emphasizes the sudden and radical character of the alteration of perspective induced in the minister and strongly looks forward to the sudden and radical *volte face* which results in his confession. The narrator's explanation of the transformations as the result of "the minister's own will, and Hester's will, and the fate that grew between them" fits into the ambiguity of the pattern first by suggesting the conflict between Hester's strong will to perpetuate his falsehood and his own weak will to tell the truth, and second, by implying concreteness in the vagueness of its third element, "the fate that grew between them." There is nothing to preclude the conception of this "fate" as Pearl. The explanation may be so construed as to suggest a double meaning in the term *transformation* and to include a double set of agents operative in effecting the change: Dimmesdale's and Hester's plans transforming Dimmesdale into a new and spuriously free man; Pearl's rejection transforming Dimmesdale into a really free man. In this second sense, there is nothing to preclude the operation of Pearl as an efficient cause of the change effected in Dimmesdale between the moment of his meeting Hester and the child in the forest and the moment of his voluntary mounting of the pillory to declare his guilt to the world—"the same minister returned not from the forest." Ostensibly, a morally worse minister returned. Actually, as the final pillory scene shows, a morally better minister returned. . . .

In a passage which concludes the homeward walk, the narrator emphasizes the lack of self-understanding which marks this stage of the transformation in Dimmesdale. In passionate self-address, the tormented man questions himself as to the possibility of his being mad, or leagued with the devil, who now demands evil deeds of his victim. . . .

On the literal, factual, narrative level, this account of manifestations of change in Dimmesdale is pejorative [belittling]. But on the figurative level, the opposite interpretation is possible and valid in the light of both antecedent and subsequent action. "Another man had returned from the forest. . . ." It may be a man enlightened by subtly communicated knowledge of "hidden mysteries which the simplicity of the former could never have reached." This knowledgeable man may well "stand apart from that former self [i.e., the pious hypocrite] eyeing it with scornful, pitying, but half-envious curiosity.". . .

DIMMESDALE TAKES ACTION AT LAST

The complete destruction of the first Election Sermon, conceived and written in deceit and hypocrisy, may be significant of a complete break with the past that produced it. The fluent composition of a new one may figure the tremendous vitality of the soul freed from the shackles of sin and operating under the flow of divine grace. As his physical appetite is satisfied by his ravenous eating, so the appetite of his soul now seems to satiate itself in ecstatic composition that continues unabated throughout the night and ceases only when the morning sun throws a golden beam into the study and lays it "right across the minister's bedazzled eyes." The sun image recalls the forest scene. Is it a figure of the new light that shone upon the darkened soul of the sensitive minister as he saw his little daughter standing in a shaft of sunlight in the gloomy forest—the only ray of light in that wilderness—and recognized in her, however obscurely at first, the prophet of his transformation and redemption?

The answer lies in the final scene at the pillory on Election Sermon Day, the scene for which the narrator has provided through the artistic device of ambiguity in three stages, those of Preparation, Communication, and Transformation. They have led inexorably to the fourth—Revelation. . . . The opening paragraphs of the next chapter (Chap. XXIII)—those in which the narrator describes the general effect of the sermon—suggest that the sound [of Dimmesdale's voice] conveyed to her the sense of an ending and a beginning: the ending of their plans for escape (indeed, she already knows that Chillingworth has outwitted her, although Dimmesdale does not know it) and the beginning of a new phase in the minister's life, not that which her will has planned, but another over which she has no control, for it involves his death.

Hester is well aware that she is seeing and hearing a Dimmesdale who is radically different from the Dimmesdale of the forest. She does not know the cause of the change in him. But I suggest that Dimmesdale now knows. It is Pearl. From the moment of her dramatic rejection of him in the forest, he has moved in bewilderment and agony at the conflict within him towards this moment when he will identify her as his daughter to the world. Refusing all human aid except that of the woman who wears the sign of his sin, he stands at the foot of the scaffold and, at the very moment of confession, summons Pearl, his child. This time she does not refuse. . . .

When the "dreadful witness" of his sin, his scarlet letter, has been exposed, it is to Pearl that the dying man speaks. He asks her for a kiss, the sign of reconciliation that she had refused him in the forest. Her response is immediate and wholehearted. . . .

PEARL ACCOMPLISHES HER MISSION

From the very beginning the narrator has made clear the nature of Pearl's mission to her mother: she had been sent as a blessing and as a retribution to remind Hester of her fall from grace and to teach her the way to heaven. Her mission to her father, however, has been a hidden one. . . . It is unthinkable that an artist of the stature of Nathaniel Hawthorne should fail to motivate the central action of his most distinguished and most admired work. There must be a cause for Dimmesdale's confession. It is Pearl in her preternatural aspect.

Hester's Defiance

Nina Baym

Nina Baym, professor of English at the University of
Illinois at Urbana and author of essays on feminist
literary criticism, takes a feminist approach in her
analysis of *The Scarlet Letter.* Baym emphasizes that
Hester, with her creative needlework, is an artist living in a society that "does not recognize and provide
for imaginative expression." In this rigidly restrictive
community she can express herself only with her
needlework.

In *The Scarlet Letter* Hawthorne defined the focus of all four
of his completed long romances: the conflict between passionate, self-assertive, and self-expressive inner drives and
the repressing counterforces that exist in society and are
also internalized within the self. In this romance he also
formulated some of the recurrent elements in his continuing
exploration of this theme. In Hester he developed the first of
a group of female representatives of the human creative and
passionate forces, while in Dimmesdale he created the first
of several guilt-prone males, torn between rebellious and
conforming impulses. These two characters operate in *The
Scarlet Letter* in a historical setting, which was not repeated
in any of Hawthorne's later romances, but the historical setting is shaped according to thematic preoccupations that do
recur. Nominally Puritan, the society in *The Scarlet Letter* in
fact symbolizes one side of the conflict. . . .

HAWTHORNE'S TREATMENT OF THE PURITANS

In *The Scarlet Letter,* unlike Hawthorne's stories about Ann
Hutchinson, the Quakers, Roger Williams, or the Salem
witches, the Puritans are not punishing a heresy but an act
that in its essence does not appear to quarrel with Puritan
doctrine. What Hester and Dimmesdale have done is not a
crime against belief but against the law. Many critics have

Excerpted from *The Shape of Hawthorne's Career* by Nina Baym, pp. 124–42. Copyright
©1976 by Cornell University. Used by permission of the publisher, Cornell University
Press.

maintained that, since the act violates one of the Ten Commandments, it is necessarily seen by Hawthorne as a crime against Divine Law. But in *The Scarlet Letter* he considers the act entirely as a social crime. Precisely because he does not take up the issue of whether the law broken is a divine law, the issues center on the relations of Hester and Dimmesdale to their community and to themselves as they accept or deny the judgment of the community on them. They differ from one another, not as beings more or less religious, more or less "saved," but as beings differently bound to the community and differently affected by it.

Such a thematic situation is created in *The Scarlet Letter* by the virtual absence of God from the text, and in this respect the romance is a very poor representation of the Puritan mental life as the Puritan himself would have experienced it. Divinity in this romance is a remote, vague, ceremonially invoked concept that functions chiefly to sanction and support the secular power of the Puritan rulers. And—another difference from Hawthorne's earlier formulation of Puritan psychology—these rulers are not transfigured by the zeal of a recovered faith burning like a lamp in their hearts. Remove the sense of communal purpose and service in behest of God, and a self-satisfied secular autocracy remains; this is what we find in *The Scarlet Letter.* The Puritans of this community are sagacious, practical, realistic; they are lovers of form and display; they even tend toward luxury—consider Hester's many opportunities for fancy embroidery, and the elegance of Governor Bellingham's residence.

THE RULING ELDERS

The ruling group is composed of old males, aptly epitomized in the Governor, "a gentleman advanced in years, and with a hard experience written in his wrinkles. He was not ill fitted to be the head and representative of a community, which owed its origin and progress, and its present state of development, not to the impulses of youth, but to the stern and tempered energies of manhood, and the sombre sagacity of age; accomplishing so much, precisely because it imagined and hoped so little." This patriarchy surrounds itself with displays of power, and when Hawthorne writes that this was "a period when the forms of authority were felt to possess the sacredness of divine institutions," he makes the point, crucial for his story, that the Puritans venerate authority, not because it is an instrument in God's service, but because they believe secular authority itself to be divine.

What Hawthorne says of this group at the beginning of the romance he repeats at the end. In the final scene we see them as men of "long-tried integrity," of "solid wisdom and sad-colored experience," with "endowments of that grave and weighty order, which gives the idea of permanence, and comes under the general definition of respectability." The portrait is by no means wholly unfavorable (although respectable or authoritarian types will become increasingly unattractive in the subsequent romances) because Hawthorne feels, as he felt in *Grandfather's Chair,* that men of this type were required to establish a new nation: "They had fortitude and self-reliance, and, in time of difficulty or peril, stood up for the welfare of the state like a line of cliffs against a tempestuous tide." But such men are totally unfit to "meddle with a question of human guilt, passion, and anguish"—to meddle, that is, with the private, inner, imaginative life of the person. They are purely formal, purely public men; the society they devise accordingly recognizes no private life, and it is against this obtuseness that Hester and Dimmesdale must try to understand their own behavior and feelings.

HESTER, DIMMESDALE, AND PEARL

A community that embodies the qualities of aging public males must necessarily repress those of the young and female. Dimmesdale is a brilliant young minister who, in order to maintain himself as a favorite among the oligarchs, has repressed himself—made himself prematurely old by resolutely clinging to childhood. He "trode in the shadowy by-paths, and thus kept himself simple and childlike; coming forth, when occasion was, with a freshness, and fragrance, and dewy purity of thought, which, as many people said, affected them like the speech of an angel." In this dewy innocent we recognize faint traces of Hawthorne's earlier men of fancy, and like them Dimmesdale does not so much want power as approval. He is a dependent personality. But he is still a young man, and to forgo the engagement with life characteristic of youth he must continually hold himself back. His "sin" is an impulsive relaxation of self-restraint and a consequent assertion of his youthful energies against the restrictions established by the elders. He does a passionate, thoughtless, willful thing. Precipitated out of his protected security as much by fear as by guilt, he must now confront the conflicts of adulthood. It is not only that he has been initiated into sex; it is less the sexual than the mental and emotional that interests Hawthorne, the inner rather than the outer aspects of the experience. Dimmesdale must now recognize and deal with previously hidden, subversive, and disobedient parts of himself.

Hester begins from no such position of security as Dimmesdale, and her relative lack of protection is at once a disadvantage and a blessing. He is the darling insider while she is in many ways an outsider even before her deed exposes her to public disgrace. She has been sent to Massachusetts by her husband, there to await his arrival; her own will is not implicated in her residence in the community. She thus has nothing like Dimmesdale's tie to the group at the outset. If, as the unfolding of the romance demonstrates, she is a far more independent character than Dimmesdale, her independence may be partly the effect of her relative unimportance in and to society and her consequent paradoxical freedom within it. To judge by the development of a certain feminist ideology in Hester's thinking over the years, it would seem that Hawthorne intended to represent a basic difference in the status of men and women within a patriarchal structure. Since women are of less account than men— are not fully members of the society—they are coerced physically rather than psychologically. Forced to wear a symbol of shame in public, Hester is left alone behind that symbol to develop as she will.

The story of *The Scarlet Letter* evolves from the sin of omission that has occurred before the narrative begins to a much more important sin of commission that takes place in the same place seven years later. The original sexual encounter between Hester and Dimmesdale was an act neither of deliberate moral disobedience nor of conscious social rebellion. The characters had forgotten society and were thinking only of themselves. But seven years later when they meet again, they deliberately reject the judgment society has passed upon them. "What we did had a consecration of its own," Hester says, and "what hast thou to do with all these iron men, and their opinions?" Deciding to leave the community, they in effect deny its right to punish them. Hester is

mainly responsible for this decision; seven years of solitude
have made of her a rebel and a radical. The consequent cat-
astrophe originates with Dimmesdale, whose fragile personality cannot sustain the posture of defiance once Hester's
support has been removed and he is back in the community.
He reverts—rather quickly—to the view that society has the
right to judge and therefore that its judgment is right. His
dying speech does not convince Hester. "Is not this better,"
he demands, "than what we dreamed of in the forest?" "I
know not! I know not!" she replies. She undertakes alone
the journey they had planned together and secures the fruit
of her sin from the consequences of a Puritan judgment.
Then, surprisingly, she returns.

But by returning, even though she takes up the scarlet letter and wears it until her death, she does not acknowledge
her guilt. Rather, she admits that the shape of her life has
been determined by the interaction between that letter, the
social definition of her identity, and her private attempt to
withstand that definition. . . . But by again wearing the letter
after her return—a gesture nobody would have required of
her after so many years—and thus bringing the community
to accept that letter on her terms rather than its own, Hester
has in fact brought about a modest social change. Society expands to accept her with the letter—the private life carves
out a small place for itself in the community's awareness.
This is a small, but real, triumph for the heroine. . . .

For the seven solitary years that she remains in the community, Hester tries to come to terms with its judgment. She
actually wants to accept that judgment, for, if she can, she
will see purpose and meaning in her suffering. But her attempts cannot shake her deepest conviction that she has not
sinned—that is, that the social judgment is not a divine judgment: "Man had marked this woman's sin by a scarlet letter,
which had such potent and disastrous efficacy that no
human sympathy could reach her, save it were sinful like
herself. God, as a direct consequence of the sin which man
thus punished, had given her a lovely child, whose place
was on that same dishonored bosom, to connect her parent
for ever with the race and descent of mortals, and to be finally a blessed soul in heaven!"

As an embodiment of Hester's sin, Pearl is a kind of vari-
ant of the scarlet letter. Hester perceives her as such, and
dresses her to bring out the identity, "arraying her in a crim-

son velvet tunic, of a peculiar cut, abundantly embroidered with fantasies and flourishes of gold thread. . . . It was a remarkable attribute of this garb, and indeed, of the child's whole appearance, that it irresistibly and inevitably reminded the beholder of the token which Hester Prynne was doomed to wear upon her bosom. It was the scarlet letter in another form; the scarlet letter endowed with life!" In dressing Pearl to look like the letter, Hester appears to be trying to accept the Puritan idea that Pearl is a creature of guilt. But her behavior is subversive and cunning, for she has already transformed the letter into a work of art with her gorgeous embroidery, and it is to this transfigured symbol that she matches Pearl.

THE IMPORTANCE OF HESTER'S ART

Hester's art—and that she is an artist, Hawthorne leaves no doubt—though ornamental in form, must not be confused with the delicate prettiness of Owen Warland's butterfly or the cold fragility of the snow-image. Her art is not pretty but splendid, and not cold but fiercely passionate, for it stems directly from the passionate self that engendered Pearl and is now denied all other expression: "She had in her nature a rich, voluptuous, Oriental characteristic,—a taste for the gorgeously beautiful, which, save in the exquisite productions of her needle, found nothing else, in all the possibilities of her life, to exercise itself upon." Now this expressive activity, which is fundamentally nonsocial, must be realized in shapes that are perceived and classified and judged by society. Hester's activity is permissible when it is employed in giving "majesty to the forms in which a new government manifested itself to the people," that is, by creating "deep ruffs, painfully wrought bands, and gorgeously embroidered gloves." With these items her gift is brought into the service of authority. But when Hester employs this same activity on her own letter, it is quite another matter. By making the letter beautiful, Hester is denying its literal meaning and thereby subverting the intention of the magistrates who condemn her to wear it. Moreover, by applying this art to her own letter, she puts her gift to work in the service of her private thoughts and feelings rather than in support of public rituals. The Puritan women understand at once what she has done: "She hath good skill at her needle, that's certain . . . but did ever a woman, before this brazen hussy, contrive such a way of showing it! Why, gossips, what is it but to laugh in the faces of our godly magistrates, and make a pride out of what they, worthy gentlemen, meant for a punishment?" Fortunately for Hester—fortunately for the artist—the magistrates lack this ironic perception. They are not imaginative men, and if this failing has led them to deny expression to the imagination, it also prevents them from recognizing it when it manifests itself in subtle or indirect forms.

HESTER'S PLACE IN THE COMMUNITY

But in a society that does not recognize and provide forms for imaginative expression, the artist of the private must always make her statement covertly by distorting the available public forms of expression. The executed product therefore involves a compromise, sometimes a very radical one, between the conception and its final shape. In the interplay between Pearl and the letter, Hawthorne and Hester both wrestle with the problem of bringing together the artist's "idea," which is nonsocial and even nonverbal, and the eventual product. At the most basic level the writer must use language, a social construct, for his expression. Thereby his product becomes social even if his idea is not. Pearl, the antisocial creature, must be transformed into the letter *A*. Ultimately, artistic conceptions that are expressive but perhaps not meaningful in a declarative sense must acquire meanings through the form in which they are expressed. . . . The undecorated scarlet letter would certainly be a form false to Hester's conception of what she has done. Her recourse is to play with that form in order to loosen it, expand it, undercut it, and thereby make it capable of a sort of many-layered communication. Her artist's activity is directly contrasted to the operation of the Puritan mind, forever anxiously codifying the phenomena of its world into the rigid system of its alphabet.

If Pearl is Hester's imagination of her sin, she also symbolizes the sinful part of Hester's self—the wild, amoral, creative core. Hester is at odds with this part of herself . . . and, until she comes to some sort of resolution, is a divided personality. Truly to assent to her punishment, Hester must come to judge her own nature, or that part of it, as society has judged it. She does try to feel guilty, and hopes that by behaving like a guilty person she will eventually create a sense of guilt within her. She tries to restrain and discipline the child according to society's judgments, but her passionate nature—pushed by ostracism into defiance—continues to assert itself. Pearl expresses all the resentment, pride, anger, and blasphemy that Hester feels but may not voice, and perhaps does not even admit to feeling. One recalls the famous catechism scene where Pearl, to Hester's mortification, proclaims that "she had not been made at all, but had been plucked by her mother off the bush of wild roses, that grew by the prison-door." Pearl repudiates all patriarchs: God, the magistrates, her actual father. Boldly, the child aligns her mother with the persecuted and martyred, for the rosebush is said to have sprung from the footsteps of "sainted" Ann Hutchinson. Pearl locates herself within a world inhabited entirely by women, figuring her birth as an event that occurred without men. She confirms the conflict in Hester's case as one between a woman and a patriarchal social structure....

PEARL'S UNPREDICTABLE BEHAVIOR

Although Hester tried to rear her daughter with tender yet strict discipline, Pearl's independent nature and her mercurial moods often made this difficult. This passage from The Scarlet Letter *shows why Hester sometimes wondered if Pearl was even human.*

Hester Prynne, nevertheless, the lonely mother of this one child, ran little risk of erring on the side of undue severity. Mindful, however, of her own errors and misfortunes, she early sought to impose a tender, but strict, control over the infant immortality that was committed to her charge. But the task was beyond her skill. After testing both smiles and frowns, and proving that neither mode of treatment possessed any calculable influence, Hester was ultimately compelled to stand aside, and permit the child to be swayed by her own impulses. Physical compulsion or restraint was effectual, of course, while it lasted. As to any other kind of discipline, whether addressed to her mind or heart, little Pearl might or might not be within its reach, in accordance with the caprice that ruled the moment. Her mother, while Pearl was yet an infant, grew acquainted with a certain peculiar look, that warned her when it would be labor thrown away to insist, persuade, or plead. It was a look so intelligent, yet inexplicable, so perverse, sometimes so malicious, but generally accompanied by a wild flow of spirits, that Hester could not help questioning, at such moments, whether Pearl was a human child.

Alone, [Hester's] emotions repressed, she does her needle-work and thinks. She "assumed a freedom of speculation . . . which our forefathers, had they known of it, would have held to be a deadlier crime than that stigmatized by the scarlet let-ter." Had she spoken her thoughts, she probably would "have suffered death from the stern tribunals of the period, for attempting to undermine the foundations of the Puritan establishment." Naturally, her mind dwells much on her condition as a woman, especially because caring for a girl-child forces her to see her situation in more general terms: "Was existence worth accepting, even to the happiest among [women]?" Pursuing her thought, she is overwhelmed by the magnitude of the changes that must occur before woman's lot becomes generally tolerable. There is certainly no indi-vidual solution; there is only individual escape into happy love. But love for Hester is the instrument of misery rather than an escape into bliss, for it is love that keeps her in Boston close to Dimmesdale all those long, sad years. And when she proposes to leave, it is not for herself but for him that she is concerned. The limitation imposed by love on freedom is an aspect of woman's (as distinct from the gen-eral human) condition, and this is partly why Hester, re-turned to Boston, hopes for the revelation of a new truth that will "establish the whole relation between man and woman on a surer ground of mutual happiness."

HESTER AND DIMMESDALE REACT DIFFERENTLY

Hester, labeled guilty by society, gradually rejects the mean-ing of that label although she cannot reject the label itself. Dimmesdale, thought to be innocent, eventually displays himself in public as a guilty man. His character contrasts completely with Hester's, except in one crucial respect: both of them must ultimately, at whatever cost, be true to the im-peratives of their own natures. No matter how she tries to assent to it, Hester cannot help but reject the judgment of the letter. Dimmesdale must finally stigmatize himself no mat-ter how much a part of him longs to concur in the idea of his innocence. As I have already briefly observed, Hester is nat-urally independent and romantic, Dimmesdale dependent and conservative, and these tendencies are reinforced by their different places in the social structure. . . .

Observe that public confession has in fact never been de-manded of Hester. She has never had to say "I am guilty," because, for the Puritans, to have done the deed and to be guilty are synonymous, and Hester has obviously done the deed. Dimmesdale has no such escape. If he confesses, he must confess his guilt. Chillingworth as a substitute for social judgment actually forestalls that judgment and protects Dimmesdale from an ultimate condemnation. Once he confesses, he has no psychological alternative but to die. Quite literally, Chillingworth the physician has kept him alive all these years, even if only to torment him. . . .

The final scene on the scaffold seems to suggest that the public institutions of society and the private needs of the personality are irreconcilable. Dimmesdale, revealing his inner nature, has died. Hester, in order to express herself at last and to permit Pearl to develop freely, must leave the community. But her return to Boston and the consequent loosening of the community to accommodate her lighten the gloomy conclusion. A painfully slow process of social relaxation may, perhaps, be hoped for. The human heart may not need to be an outcast forever.

THE PURITANS AS THE SOCIAL NORM

The Puritan community in *The Scarlet Letter* is a symbol of society in general. It is portrayed as a set of institutions unresponsive to personal needs and deliberately repressive of the private experience. Puritan institutions define the human being as all surface, all public. So far as the inner life is made public, it must be submitted to social definitions. Social institutions, however, may not be defined in the language of individual needs. The Puritan magistrates are not hypocrites. For them, the business of establishing and perpetuating a society demands the full energies of all the members of the community; there is no time for the indulgence of a private dimension of the personality. Self-expression is therefore a threat to the community.

Since the magistrates believe that self-expression is a threat, they make it a crime. Thereby, of course, they make it a threat as well. *The Scarlet Letter* asks whether this state of opposition between passion and authority is necessary; it expresses the hope that a society allowing greater individual expression might evolve, but it does not commit itself to a certain conclusion. It makes clear, however, that in a society such as the romance describes, the relationship of the artist who speaks for passion to the social institutions that suppress it can only be one of estrangement, duplicity, or subversion. Dimmesdale's voice and Hester's letter enunciate and undermine the social creed. Disguised as a social document, the work of art secretly expresses the cry of the heart. Doing this, it covertly defies society in response to hidden but universal needs.

CHAPTER 3

Major Themes

READINGS ON
THE SCARLET LETTER

Hawthorne Examines English Traditions

Frederick Newberry

To appreciate the richness of the plot of *The Scarlet Letter*, the reader must grasp the secondary motifs that Hawthorne weaves into the story. One such motif is the difference between the culture and values of the Old World English and the New World Puritans' rejection of the same. To Hawthorne, the breach that separated the aesthetics and humanity of the two groups was as wide as the ocean that separated them. In the following essay, Hawthorne scholar Frederick Newberry expounds on the cultural differences of the Old and New World residents and relates them to the main theme and to the characters.

Although Hawthorne's indignation over being dismissed from his post is embedded in "The Custom-House" [the introduction to *The Scarlet Letter*], a crucial element of that indignation finds expression in a historical perspective that both includes and transcends Hawthorne's personal case. A Jonathan Pue, a [Geoffrey] Chaucer, or a [Robert] Burns could rely on the traditional support of his government and culture. England had a history of valuing its artists, while America did not. The recognition was not new to Hawthorne, but he experienced it now more fully and personally than earlier; and in so doing he discovered the subject necessary for the novel that had so long eluded him: the very origins of anti-aesthetic, anti-imaginative prejudice of New England. Lying at the heart of *The Scarlet Letter*, therefore, exists a fairly large measure of hostility aimed at Puritan America's conventional mistrust of art. More fully articulated than in previous works, such mistrust went hand in hand with the cultural separation between New and Old Worlds. And more fully evident than heretofore appears a di-

Excerpted from *Hawthorne's Divided Loyalties: England and America in His Works* by Frederick Newberry (Rutherford, NJ: Fairleigh Dickinson University Press, 1987). Copyright ©1987 by Associated University Presses, Inc. Reprinted by permission.

vision in Hawthorne's loyalties to these separate worlds because of his determination to recover an English aesthetic for himself and America. . . .

Nevertheless, more cogently than in Hawthorne's previous work, *The Scarlet Letter* is about the cultural history of Puritan America, and the conflict between dominant and recessive qualities of Puritanism more or less defined by 1649. As Hawthorne sees it, the seven-year period covered by the novel's action is pivotal, not only in New England history but also, and most relevantly, in English history. With his knowledge of colonial American history, in conjunction with his considerable knowledge of English history, Hawthorne again traces the growth of the dominating forces of Puritanism: severity, rigidity, intolerance, iconoclasm, militancy, and persecution. But he also explores to a far greater extent than earlier the attractive but recessive qualities of early Puritans that form a part of their English heritage: sympathy, charity, gaiety, communal celebration, respect for tradition, and appreciation of art. These qualities—personified especially by Dimmesdale, Hester, and Pearl—are posed as alternatives to the dominant traits of the Puritan majority. Linked with English antiquity, these alternatives, if they had flourished in the New World, would have given an entirely different tone and direction to New England and thus to American history as a whole.

Presenting the dominant and recessive dualism as a historical principle and using it as a structuring device, Hawthorne substantially retraces the design of his seventeenth-century tales. The gentle side of Puritanism retreats as the militant side continually advances. Moreover, Hawthorne takes up in *The Scarlet Letter* where he leaves off in "The Custom-House," allying himself with an English ancestry whose aesthetic and spiritual traditions are pitted against those of his Puritan forebears, which essentially survive among his contemporaries. While the dominant values of the Puritans are not wholly those of nineteenth-century Salemites, the recessive values in each century are nearly identical as expressed through Hawthorne's self-projected narrator. The majority parties of the seventeenth and nineteenth centuries are oppressive in their own ways, as they resist or fail to consider either the value of art or alternatives to the narrow Puritan tradition. The legacy of Puritan antipathy for artistic values survives in nineteenth-century descendants, even though religious zeal does not. When Hawthorne adopts an English ancestry and aesthetic heritage in "The Custom-House," when he creates the artistically beautiful scarlet letter and commits himself to writing a novel on the historical and symbolic importance of this artifact, he clearly takes a positive stand at once against the dominating values of his contemporaries and his ancestors. At the outset of *The Scarlet Letter*, something antagonistic figures in Hawthorne's motives in writing on a Puritanical animus [spirit] for art and the individualistic spirit of artists. Perhaps he does ally himself to the antinomian [the belief that faith alone will bring salvation] tradition of Anne Hutchinson.

A measure of this antagonism appears directly or implicitly in repeated parallels between English culture and the New England scene. Underlying the primary attention given to New England history in the novel, there resides a subsurface of English history that Hawthorne has carefully structured in order to examine American Puritans within a framework larger than the provincial boundaries of New England. This subsurface of English history alternately interpenetrates the condition, consciousness, and subconsciousness of that early group of Puritan immigrants comprising the Great Migration. Hawthorne's sensitivity to the tension fostered by Massachusetts's quarrel with and dependence on the mother country finally amounts to one of the novel's chief imaginative distinctions. For *The Scarlet Letter* stands alone in American literary history as the only major novel directly concentrating on the seventeenth-century historical transition between Old and New Worlds, as if Hawthorne had come to believe that native literature could have little if any foundation unless the process and results of this transition were adequately examined. Given Hawthorne's treatment of early Puritan culture, the dynamics of this shift must necessarily constitute the endowed basis of both American history and art.

PURITANS RENOUNCE ENGLISH HERITAGE

References to an English heritage in *The Scarlet Letter* therefore combine to establish a rich cultural lineage available to the Puritans as part of their English birthright. Yet they try their utmost to disguise or deny this very lineage. As "The May-pole of Merry Mount" has forecast, historical continuities, communal relations, traditional festivals—all of England's hereditary customs celebrating life and community relations—are transformed or virtually rejected by Puritan emigrants. The best aesthetic qualities inextricably tied to the English church and, farther back, to the Catholic Church suffer a similar fate. Even worse, the ancient respect for these qualities is left behind, for the most part, in the mother country. *The Scarlet Letter* thus centers on a period in American history when leading forces of Puritanism—the vanguard, to Hawthorne, of the notorious second generation of Puritans—are on the verge of totally disinheriting themselves from the richest traditions of their past. Hawthorne's evocation of these traditions, as they existed at a critical moment in seventeenth-century history when they might have been nourished, casts into relief the instituted severity and barrenness of Puritan culture.

The Puritans' confrontation with the American wilderness accounts for only a small portion of the transformation of English customs and aesthetic values. As the second paragraph of the novel suggests, the Puritans had from the outset a mistaken conception of their Utopian enterprise. . . . Something intrinsically uncharitable and iconoclastic lay deep in Puritanism itself. Whether in England or in America, Puritans were engaged in a process of cultural self-disinheritance. The relationship between English and American Puritans is surely not an especially obvious one in *The Scarlet Letter.* Simply by taking note of the novel's time frame (1642–49), however, one quickly realizes the connection. In light of other signal details in the book, it becomes clear that Hawthorne has purposely structured the chronology of *The Scarlet Letter* to coincide with that of the English Civil War. The hyperbolic [excessive] revolutionary climate of presidential elections in "The Custom-House" becomes a counterpart to revolutionary change in *The Scarlet Letter.*

Effects of the English Civil War

The significance of this historical parallel can hardly be overestimated. For if one considers the novel with the English Civil War in mind, along with references and allusions to earlier epochs of English history, then the subject of historical alienation found in the book assumes a dimension far greater than a privileged focus on New England allows. Hawthorne, adopting a sweeping historical view, suggests that this alienation includes the breach between past and present in both the Old and New Worlds. In a manner analogous to the strategy in "The Old Manse," he enlarges the provincial dimensions of his American setting with imagery attached to traditions in England, suggesting evaluative comparisons for judging American history and culture—often with ironic, paradoxical, damning, and sad reflections on American Puritanism. Hawthorne indeed becomes "the historian of the historically disinherited," but in more sweeping cultural terms than have been recognized.

The time frame of *The Scarlet Letter* can most easily be determined from the reference in chapter 12 to John Winthrop's death, which took place in 1649, and from the numerous references to the scaffold scene that opens the novel seven years earlier. Since the novel begins in 1642 before news of the Civil War has reached Massachusetts, it is appropriate that when the beadle ushers Hester out of prison, he cries aloud to the crowd surrounding the door, "'Make way, good people, make way, in the King's name.'" No further allusion to Charles I appears until chapter 13, following mention of Winthrop's death in the previous chapter and thus chronologically following the execution of Charles I on 30 January 1649. Hawthorne then appropriately alludes to regicide in a passage relating to Hester and a schism in the traditional hierarchy: "It was an age in which the human intellect, newly emancipated, had taken a more active and a wider range than for many centuries before. Men of the sword had overthrown nobles and kings." Ambiguous though the plural "kings" seems to be, no monarch other than Charles I was overthrown during the age, a fact known to a writer as widely read as Hawthorne in British and European history. . . .

PARALLEL CHANGES IN ENGLAND AND NEW ENGLAND

By recalling customs and festivals evolved from English antiquity, and by setting *The Scarlet Letter* during the years of the Civil War, Hawthorne takes advantage of contrasting versions of England. Both versions are necessary to illuminate the historical conditions of New England upon which he most obviously focuses. With these dual versions of England in the background, several issues in *The Scarlet Letter* become especially meaningful.

By way of preface, a few additional details help to clarify the overall historical context within which Hawthorne explores such issues as the relationship between past and present, the role of art in conflict with Puritan iconoclasm, the religious conflict within Dimmesdale, the relation between Dimmesdale and other Puritan leaders, and the ironic concluding promise of a glorious future for America. In England, the religious tensions between the English Church and Puritans, along with political tensions between the monarchy and Parliament, reach a breaking point between 1642 and 1649. Puritan forces gradually assume power, overthrowing the monarchy and episcopacy. As the old order declines in England during these years, so too does it decline among the first generation of American Puritans—a generation having emigrated because of the increasing tensions in England, without altogether having denied the heritage of the mother country. The characteristics of the old orders in England and America are certainly not equivalent, yet they do resemble each other compared to the more militant and iconoclastic forms of Puritanism that replace them. Just as the representative of the old order in England dies in the person of Charles I, so the representative of the first generation of American Puritans dies in the person of Winthrop (and, in his symbolic role in *The Scarlet Letter*, in the person of Dimmesdale). And just as [Oliver] Cromwell assumes command of England after Charles I, so the militant Endicott takes charge of the second generation in New England after Winthrop. The break with tradition and its patriarchal leadership is completed both between and within the Old and New Worlds.

HESTER AND PEARL

[In] *The Scarlet Letter*... separate characters embody the dominant and the recessive (but attractive) sides of Puritanism. The novel... places in the foreground the figures who are to recede from American history—Hester with her luxuriant Renaissance-style artistry; Pearl, the symbol of that art; and Dimmesdale with his influential power of sympathy. These characters are particularly anomalous in the Puritan setting of the novel; Hawthorne must imaginatively create them in order to counter the harsh historical forces represented to some degree by Governor Bellingham and, less overtly but far more importantly, by Endicott, who is almost entirely offstage yet ready to make his entrance as the action of *The Scarlet Letter* concludes on election day. As Endicott comes to power, Dimmesdale dies and Hester and Pearl remove themselves from the New World. Pearl is altogether lost to America, while Hester returns appreciably altered in character. Through these figures, preeminently, *The Scarlet Letter* dramatizes mitigating alternatives to Puritanic militancy, persecution, and iconoclasm. It is clearly no accident that these appealing figures are lost to the colony, for the same pattern of survival and loss extends to minor figures, including the gentlest of the women watching Hester's disgrace at the novel's opening: unlike the bloodthirsty "gossips," she is dead in the final scene seven years later.

The qualities that recede include aesthetic sensibility, tenderness, and, on a broader scale, a sense of time-honored communal relations uniting past and present. Hawthorne had factual warrant for claiming the one-time existence of these alternatives to Puritanic extremism: the "not unkind," sometimes temperate John Wilson is a historical figure partly analogous, in the book, to Dimmesdale; and King's Chapel, reviving English tradition in America later in the seventeenth century, does stand in modern Boston by what Hawthorne fictionally designates as the burial ground of Dimmesdale himself. But Hester's art evidently has no historical counterpart; thus, as in "The Custom-House," Hawthorne has created it without reference to an actual source. Nevertheless, his eclectic use of historical background in presenting Hester, Pearl, and, especially, Dimmesdale deserves more than passing consideration.

DIMMESDALE

The Scarlet Letter places Renaissance color and love of exotic beauty, embodied by Hester and Pearl, in striking relief against the stark, joyless modes and manners of the Puritan majority. Similarly, it shows that Dimmesdale is all that the Puritan magistrates are not. While it is true that his character and actions are rendered somewhat ambiguous by his sin of adultery and especially by his failure to confess it, it is Dimmesdale who, on occasion with Wilson, tempers the severe judgments of Bellingham and others. Not only do his peers and superiors listen respectfully to him (Wilson finds him "wise beyond his years"), but also the people respond to him with the sympathy that he alone seems able to draw from them. His inability to aid Hester and, worse, to be a father to Pearl surely troubles a modern reader—but we should note that for other parishioners he serves as a comforting confessor and spiritual advisor: "his heart vibrated in unison with theirs, and received their pain into itself." His sympathetic powers clearly distinguish Dimmesdale from the other clergymen who are "endowed with a far greater share of shrewd, hard, iron or granite understanding; which, duly mingled with a fair proportion of doctrinal ingredient, constitutes a highly respectable, efficacious, and unamiable variety of the clerical species." The lack of amiability characterizes virtually all the Puritan clergy, save Dimmesdale.

Just as Hester and Pearl are in continuous conflict with the entire populace, so Dimmesdale is pitted throughout the novel against more particularized forces of persecution: Chillingworth's Old World science and scholarship turned diabolic; Bellingham's outward displays of gentility but inner Puritanic intolerance; and, implicitly, Endicott's militant separatism in relation to English heritage. Hawthorne regularly surrounds Hester, Pearl, and Dimmesdale with Old World motifs—often Anglo-Catholic or Renaissance images—not, of course, to make them Anglicans but to differentiate them from the other Puritans and to emphasize positive historical and cultural continuities, once potentially available to America through them.

THE AESTHETIC TRADITION

As Hester stands on the scaffold, feeling the "heavy weight of a thousand unrelenting eyes" staring at the scarlet *A* on her breast, her "memory" involuntarily revives: "Reminiscences, the most trifling and immaterial, passages of infancy and schooldays, sports, childish quarrels, and the little domestic traits of her maiden years, came swarming back upon her, intermingled with recollections of whatever was gravest in her subsequent life." Similar to Hawthorne in "The Custom-House," Hester recalls her past to gain relief "from the cruel weight and hardness of reality." She remembers her "native village, in Old England, and her paternal home; a decayed house of gray stone, with a poverty-stricken aspect, but retaining a half-obliterated shield of arms over the portal, in token of antique gentility." She also recalls her marriage to Chillingworth and their initial move to Amsterdam among "huge cathedrals, and the public edifices, ancient in date and quaint in architecture.". . .

Her English past and the optimism suggested in her duplication of the Pilgrim moves to Holland and America vividly contrast with "the rude market-place of the Puritan settlement" where, upon the scaffold, she stands holding Pearl, her public sin and perhaps her private shame exposed. Hester has been influenced with a sufficient amount of Calvinistic doctrine to feel that "the scaffold of the pillory was a point of view that revealed . . . the entire track along which she had been treading, since her happy infancy." So much for sloughing the skin of Old World corruption in coming to the New World. But while Hester acknowledges her predetermined reenactment of original sin, she evidently has not observed the orthodox logic of how she ought to behave as a result of it. She has clearly spent her months in prison in rather unrepentant and even heretical fashion. As Hester stands exposed before her neighbors in all the beauty of her person, dress, and scarlet letter, she reveals something quite different from evidentiary Puritan atonement, something far more in keeping with her Old World reflections.

HESTER REFLECTS THE OLD WORLD

In view of Puritan sumptuary laws prohibiting the general populace from wearing lavish dress, and from the vantage of Puritan opposition to religious images, Hawthorne describes Hester's appearance and the effects of her needlework in terms anomalous to the historical setting. He continues to associate her with the Old World and, more specifically, with its aristocratic (even ecclesiastical) art, presumably inimical to Puritanism. Hester, we later learn, has "fingers that could have embroidered a monarch's robe." Through the artful stitching witnessed in the scarlet letter, she produces a "specimen of her delicate and imaginative skill of which the dames of a court might gladly have availed themselves to add the richer and more spiritual adornment of human ingenuity to their fabrics of silk and gold."

The beautiful artifact initially repels the colonists, who later persecute Hester and ostracize her from the community not only because she has sinned but also because she has created a distinctly non-Puritan form of beauty from the symbol of her sin. Given the Calvinistic side of her ruminations, Hester should have expected nothing less, and so it would seem that she contributes to her own alienation. She has fashioned "wild" and "picturesque" clothing, and she has also embroidered the scarlet letter with an artistic "luxuriance of fancy." Together, these products of her skill and imagination have "a splendor in accordance with the taste of the age, but greatly beyond what was allowed by the sumptuary regulations of the colony." Some of the spectators obviously make no mistake in thinking that Hester "make[s] a pride out what" the magistrates "meant for a punishment."

From a Puritan point of view of providential signs, Hester's confinement in the dark jail should have allowed enough time for her beauty to fade and for guilt to shadow forth its physical effects. But her appearance belies these unsanctified effects anticipated by those Puritans "who had before known her, and had expected to behold her dimmed and obscured by a disastrous cloud." Instead, they are "astonished, and even startled, to perceive how her beauty shone out, and made a halo of misfortune and ignominy in which she was enveloped." Preconceptions give way to uncomfortable perceptions; and the Puritans have every reason to be alarmed over what they see. As if illuminated by the traditional aureole in Christian art and "transfigured" by the scarlet letter, Hester appears before the crowd as if in resemblance of a once-revered icon, but now an idolatrous image of the Virgin Mary. The historical moment of transition from Old to New World is the crucial context. Like John Wilson, the assembled Puritans have been "nurtured at the rich bosom of the English Church." They are accordingly familiar with the Roman Catholic imagery in the churches having survived destruction under Edward VI and in those having been readorned under James I and Charles I. What they sense in Hester's image is partly what they abhor in the Church of England: the religious art that to their minds constitutes not only idolatrous images but threatening signs of a renewed affiliation with Rome on the part of the Stuarts.

ANGLO-CATHOLIC IMAGERY

Beautiful, illuminated, and "transfigured"—her sin notwithstanding—Hester appears before the Puritans as if mocking their severe religious and aesthetic sensibilities. But at the same time, because of her sin, she poses as a shameful contrast to the traditional image her appearance suggests:

> Had there been a Papist among the crowd of Puritans, he might have seen in this beautiful woman, so picturesque in her attire and mien, and with the infant at her bosom, an object to remind him of the image of Divine Maternity, which so

many illustrious painters have vied with one another to represent; something which should remind him, indeed, but only by contrast, of that sacred image of sinless motherhood, whose infant was to redeem the world. Here, there was the taint of deepest sin in the most sacred quality of human life, working such effect, that the world was only the darker for this woman's beauty, and the more lost for the infant that she had borne.

The introduction of a Roman Catholic point of view, no more anomalous than historically resonant, temporarily completes the aesthetic resemblance Hester and Pearl bear to the Virgin Mary and Christ. Hawthorne then safely denies the suitability of the resemblance by accentuating Hester's sin. Still, we are left with uncomfortable dualisms of purity and sin, redemption and damnation, which, as it turns out, interlock in a paradoxical image symbolizing the spiritual and historical complexities at issue throughout the novel.

The Anglo-Catholic imagery associated with Hester and her art does not entirely disappear following the evocation of Madonna and Child. She exchanges her beautiful clothes for a gray robe and she hides her beautiful hair beneath a cap. Pious Bostonians, who believe in the efficacious logic of "visible sanctity," observe her "penance" and "good deeds" for seven years; and thus, by some trick of perception, memory, or Federal Theology, they come to believe that the scarlet letter has meanings other than its original designation for adultery. Even those who cannot forget the "black scandal" see with no apparent ill reflection on their divine covenant and errand that the scarlet letter "had the effect of the cross on a nun's bosom," or that it "imparted to the wearer a kind of sacredness." Altered in luxurious beauty though it is, Hester's presence somehow manages to sustain an impression "majestic and statue-like." And so from Madonna, to nun with a cross, to statue, Hester's metamorphosis retains a resemblance to icons, wholly anathema to the Puritan setting. . . . When Hester supports the fallen Dimmesdale in the last scaffold scene she once again evokes the Madonna; for their pose pictorially suggests the traditional pietà in Christian art, the whole scene having unmistakable overtones of a crucifixion.

Emphasis on these iconographical similarities further expresses the artistic side of Hester's nature, which is itself patently antipathetic to Puritan New England. There exist no religious paintings and icons in New England, and obviously there are no nuns. Before the 1640s . . . the Puritans effectively dispense with the cross as an idolatrous image belonging to Catholicism. Hawthorne certainly knew that these images were hateful anachronisms, but their ahistorical placement in the setting connects the early Puritans to their not very distant English past. Not that the colonists themselves are particularly conscious of the connection or that they would have approved of the connection had they possessed such consciousness. Hawthorne suggests instead, based upon a supposition speaking almost as much to the historical situation as it does to his own artistic needs, that beneath the iconoclastic level of consciousness the early Puritan mind remains somewhat receptive to symbols and images inherited from the Old World. Adhering to his consistent view that the past invariably exerts an influence on the present, and yet keeping within the historicity of the novel, Hawthorne does not place the image of "a nun with a cross on her bosom" directly in the minds of the Puritans, only the "effect" of that image. Hawthorne as historian and artist creates the image, because he needs the aesthetic tradition belonging to the very Anglo-Catholic theology renounced by his Puritan ancestors. . . .

PEARL

In his treatment of Pearl, Hawthorne depicts other Old World survivals in early America. When, after the novel's opening scene, Hester exchanges her dress for the gray robe, she gives her striking mode of apparel on the scaffold to Pearl. The child's dresses, made of the "richest tissues," display the aesthetic range of Hester's "imaginative faculty." Transferring the splendor of her clothes to Pearl, Hester also transfers the halo of her beauty: "So magnificent was the small figure, . . . and such was the splendor of Pearl's own proper beauty, shining through the gorgeous robes . . . that there was an absolute circle of radiance around her." Such radiance surrounds her almost everywhere in the novel, most brilliantly in the forest scene when she receives the blessing of the sun. The aureole of Christian art is once again suggested here. Notwithstanding references elsewhere to Pearl's occasional impish behavior, as she stands at the brookside wreathed in flowers, she may indeed call to mind "a medieval icon for grace.". . .

In her beauty, imaginative play, harmony with nature,

and ties with ancient traditions—all the valorized qualities carefully assembled in "The Old Manse" and "The Custom-House"—Pearl represents the best values out of which American culture might be built, the very elements missing in second-generation Puritans (and missing to a great degree in the first). Even in its childhood games, the second generation forecasts Puritanic obsessions in the latter half of the seventeenth century: "scourging Quakers; or taking scalps in a sham-fight with the Indians; or scaring one another with freaks of imitative witchcraft." That the children also play at going to church indicates with what piety they will later persecute the Quakers in the 1650s, massacre the Indians in King Philip's War [1675–1676], and convict their brethren of witchcraft in the early 1690s.

While Hawthorne introduces Pearl for multiple purposes in *The Scarlet Letter,* all of her functions seem to converge in the personification of art. Born out of sin and an extension of it, she nevertheless transcends her unholy origin. Indeed, she will grow up to become an artist in her own right when, having duly inherited Hester's talent, and having grown up somewhere in Europe within a milieu appreciative of art, she creates "beautiful tokens" with "delicate fingers." Pearl therefore embodies the powers of art as Hawthorne conceives them: beauty, intuition, morality, spirit, passion, and a respect for the aesthetic forms of the past. Worldly and spiritual truth unite at once in her, "The living hieroglyphic, . . . the character of flame.". . .

HESTER RETURNS ART TO ENGLAND

When Hester and Pearl leave New England a year after Dimmesdale's final scene on the scaffold, they take with them the aesthetic continuity between England and America that they have represented. They leave America, in other words, aesthetically barren—with the very "gap" that Hester once filled and that Pearl could one day fill in her turn. Their departure, coincident with the rise of the second generation of Puritans, suggests the magnitude of the historical schism evaluated by Hawthorne in *The Scarlet Letter.* England and Europe, not America, are cast not only as the cultural sources but also the ultimate repositories of art. Accordingly, after Hester returns to Boston some years later, she does not resume her needlework except in one instance: to embroider "a baby-garment, with such a lavish richness of golden fancy as would have raised a public tumult, had any infant, thus apparelled, been shown to our sombre-hued community." Because their origins lay in England, most first-generation Puritans could accept this form of dress in Pearl and even want to possess other articles for itself evincing Hester's art. But the second generation, led by Endicott, becomes Puritanic. Unlike its counterparts in England who experience the Restoration, it retains the iconoclastic legacy of Civil War extremists. Thus, at the novel's close, Hester must send the only expression of her art back to Europe—to Pearl and her child, symbols of a cultural transmission and of a potential artistic heritage not yet acceptable in America. The ultimate logic of Puritan severity and inconoclasm leads to restrictions altogether abortive to the development of an aesthetic tradition in the New World upon which Hawthorne and other native American artists might draw. Because he inherited an aesthetic void from New England's past, while nevertheless imagining a historical situation in which Hester could defy her persecutors and create an art constituting the basis for a tradition, it became Hawthorne's task to resurrect the tradition in his own day. His too, no less than Hester's, was a magnificent act of defiance, an assertion not only of art's legitimate place in America but also of its freedom to borrow and adapt cross-cultural traditions for reasons transcending the provincial biases of any time and place.

A Critique of Puritan Society

Alison Easton

After completing her doctoral dissertation on Hawthorne, Alison Easton wrote a book-length critique
of his collected writing. She analyzes the issues
Hawthorne raises in *The Scarlet Letter:* morality and
marriage, the nature of evil, sympathy and its ramifi-
cations, and truth. Easton contends that Hawthorne
offers no comforting panacea, but only a pattern of
resistance and accommodation to one's society.

What conclusions . . . can [*The Scarlet Letter*] offer? . . . There
is neither total freedom nor total determinism. In spite of her
subjective involvement in social structures of meaning, Hester still finds it possible to question established moral structures and to try to act upon her ideas—her envisaging a
"coming revelation" is a gesture toward change. The male
protagonists, more securely locked inside its assumptions,
destroy themselves or others. In the final scaffold scene,
"men of rank and dignity" were "perplexed as to the purport
of what they saw,—unable to receive the explanation which
most readily presented itself, or to imagine any other,—."
These men belong to a community that, for all its utopian as-
pirations, is characterized as "accomplishing so much, precisely because it imagined and hoped so little."

Hester, excluded primarily by her sex (rather than solely
by her misdemeanor) from participation in political practi-
calities of this patriarchal state, is instead partially freed to
"imagine" and "hope"—attempting creatively to visualize a
reformed social order for everyone as well as an alternative
life for Dimmesdale and herself. Perhaps it matters less that
what she wants is to make a home for Dimmesdale than that
she is capable of that initial thrust for wider change. Unlike

Reprinted from *The Making of the Hawthorne Subject* by Alison Easton, by permission
of the University of Missouri Press. Copyright ©1996 by the Curators of the University
of Missouri.

those Puritans, she has identified the centrality of changing relationships between women and men in any reformation of the community in the interests of justice and happiness. The Puritan attempt to found a better society in New England while maintaining traditional gender relations unaltered had its logical outcome in state punishment for adultery. . . . It must be noted, however, that Hester the prophetess is quite prepared to suspend her general ambitions for society in order to quit Massachusetts altogether for the arms of Dimmesdale. Her attempt to flee is doomed to failure because it is a personal solution, ignoring her knowledge of the need for wider social change.

The men, more directly implicated in power structures, find it harder to challenge them. Dimmesdale's decision to remove himself from Boston paradoxically inserts him mentally even more securely within it: he is now, in his view, a confirmed sinner and the Massachusetts colony all the more blessed in comparison. His ministerial work has shown him, like Hester, the great extent of guilt and unhappiness, but he has experienced this within an orthodox framework that submits "sinners" to their God. As a result, his glowing image of the Holy Commonwealth and its future remains untarnished by this knowledge. He certainly feels no need for radical social reform, as Hester had felt. The community loves his Election Day sermon, giving as it does such a pleasing, compensatory self-image, and so not surprisingly he thus reaches the pinnacle of his career. The euphoric sense of community caused by this political rhetoric pushes him to try to make himself fully known to it through confession. Hester was accurate in her assessment of his position in the Election Day procession—"he seemed so remote from her own sphere"—and the narrator rightly (if in a condescendingly essentialist way) sees her resentment of this as gender based: "And thus much of woman was there in Hester, that she could scarcely forgive him . . . for being able so completely to withdraw himself from their mutual world."

MORALITY AND MARRIAGE

Sexual love in this novel leads swiftly to ethical considerations, as Hester tries to evolve for herself ideas of moral right and wrong to replace demonstrably inadequate conventional structures regulating desire. Adultery may be totally prohibited—the narrator never discounts this—but the most that the novel will establish is that seventeenth-century Boston believed it to be so. Yet all three protagonists in different ways have at some point questioned this by asking what marriage means. Hester revises the old language of obligation and condemnation: "'Yes, I hate him!,'" says Hester of Chillingworth, "'He betrayed me! He has done me worse wrong than I did him!'" Negotiation between promises made to both husband and lover brings a similar shift in the symbolic system of conventional morals, made all the more vivid for Hester having to explain this change to her legal spouse: "'for, having cast off all duty towards other human beings, there remained a duty towards him [Dimmesdale]; and something whispered me that I was betraying it, in pledging myself to keep your counsel.'" It is Chillingworth who initially introduces into the discussion of morality and marriage matters of personality, circumstance, and emotion, and Hester has now extended this into what is, for both seventeenth-century and nineteenth-century institutional norms, a profoundly radical rethinking of sexual ethics. Its disruptive power is shown in the narrator's panic, seeing a world "only the darker for this woman's beauty, and the more lost for the infant that she had borne.". . .

EVIL

The exploration of moral values goes even further with speculation about what then constitutes the worst sin of all. Indeed, the clearest definition of "evil" in the novel immediately precedes that most celebrated assertion of Hester's new moral good ("'What we did had a consecration of its own. We felt it so! We said so to each other! Hast thou forgotten it?'" It is Dimmesdale who formulates the new description of sin not simply because he has experienced Chillingworth's influence most, but because he cannot shed the Puritan mentality in which the idea of "sin" plays a central role. Hester, too, in similarly seeing their situation in judgmental terms, testifies to the way her seven-year penal experience (as well as her education) has given her subjectivity a particular shape. This kind of conceptualizing (note the abstract way in which he will refer to himself) can be expected from someone who even after the forest meeting remains a minister, theologically trained to consider such questions: "'May God forgive us both! We are not, Hester, the worst sinners in the world. There is one worse than even the polluted priest!

That old man's revenge has been blacker than my sin. He has violated, in cold blood, the sanctity of a human heart. Thou and I, Hester, never did so!'" But here the idea of what constitutes the greatest evil is . . . a way of investigating the general basis of this moral shift that Hester has begun to express. So arguably the protagonists' patterns of ethical thought are here more a help than a hindrance.

The key notion here seems to be "violation," and it proves useful because it is central to all the characters and their circumstances, and relates directly to the basic conception of human subjectivity underpinning the novel. Evil is not Calvinist Original Sin, that principle of innate corruption operating within human beings. It is seen to lie in those fractures in consciousness, long since identified in Hawthorne's work as productive of suffering and a sense of wrong. Now, however, the focus is not so exclusively on the resulting pains of alienation, but on how others may exploit that gap to their own ends. "Evil" is a perversion of love (violation itself having a sexual as well as a general meaning). Both love and this "evil" involve intimacy, that access to individual subjectivity that "sympathy" makes possible. When this "heart-knowledge" constitutes an unwanted, secret, and undetected access into consciousness, then it gives the interloper power to manipulate, expose, and damage. All three protagonists recognize the potential of such knowledge: Hester had backed off in fear from the intuitions that her letter gave her about her fellow townspeople; Dimmesdale had fought not to abuse the power provided by his intimate knowledge of his parishioners; Chillingworth alone uses this power to hurt. It is a realization that leaves our somewhat conservative liberal narrator in the final chapter both fascinated by the radical implications of this for viewing the customary and far more simply conceived emotional/moral landscape of human interrelationships, and profoundly wary himself of pursuing those disruptive implications any further: "It is a curious subject of observation and inquiry, whether hatred and love be not the same thing at bottom. Each, in its utmost development, supposes a high degree of intimacy and heart-knowledge; each renders one individual dependent for the food of his affections and spiritual life upon another; each leaves the passionate lover, or the no less passionate hater, forlorn and desolate by the withdrawal of his object.". . .

VARIATIONS OF SYMPATHY

The way in which the word "sympathy" is recurrently and variously used throughout the novel further clarifies this matter. The notion of imaginative sympathy, slowly maturing over the years, clearly articulated in his Concord work but made too sweet and easy in the Salem tales, is now explored in all its complexity. The word and its derivatives occur at least forty-one times in *The Scarlet Letter,* and its significance will be distorted unless the full range of meanings is taken on board. It is not a matter of the novel merely charting its ambiguities; instead an attempt is being made to make sense of these, and to explain how it is possible for "sympathy" to lead to either trust or violation. . . .

In *The Scarlet Letter,* "sympathy" ranges across a spectrum of meaning. There is the simple and not necessarily conscious identification of like with like: the sun around Pearl "attracted thitherward as by a certain sympathy" might be a positive Romantic image, but it uncomfortably resembles another connection, this time drawn directly from Renaissance medicine, between Chillingworth and his herbs ("Would not the earth, quickened to an evil purpose by the sympathy of his eye, greet him with poisonous shrubs"). This connection can equally be pleasant or painful: the entertainers' "appeals to the very broadest sources of mirthful sympathy" are matched by a different sort of connection in which "no human sympathy could reach her [Hester], save it were sinful like herself." This may become an unwilled intuition or consciously felt link between two similarly constituted beings: the Surveyor's "mere sensuous sympathy of dust for dust" with Salem; Hester, as Pearl's mother, having "'sympathies which these men lack!'"; and the letter giving Hester "sympathetic knowledge of the hidden sin in other hearts" without any contact with them. Again, chameleonlike, one may take the color of one's surroundings: the townspeople's interest in Hester reviving "by sympathy with what they saw others feel," and Pearl's disturbed excitement an example of how "[c]hildren have always a sympathy in the agitations of those connected with them."

None of these usages has in essence a moral meaning, even if ethical implications may emerge from it. It is the narrator who leaps to a judgmental and erroneous assumption in commenting that Dimmesdale's encounter with Mistress Hibbins "did but show his sympathy and fellowship with wicked mortals and the world of perverted spirits."

True, sympathy may seem to be positive: Dimmesdale's connection with Hester makes him a better pastor, because "this very burden it was, that gave him sympathies so intimate with the sinful brotherhood of mankind; so that his heart vibrated in unison with theirs, and received their pain into itself." But there is a similar, and indeed similarly expressed, mechanism (though based on hate, not loving pity, and ultimately creating a very different outcome) operating in Chillingworth's perception of Dimmesdale's secret self: "'There is a sympathy that will make me conscious of him. I shall see him tremble. I shall feel myself shudder, suddenly and unawares.'"

MORAL IMPLICATIONS ARISE

All this merely establishes the capacity of humans to be receptive to others' emotions. Moral questions arise when consideration is made of which feelings are contacted, how this is achieved, and with what intention and what result. To be "sensitive" (a word used nine times about Dimmesdale) is a two-edged instrument. Only Chillingworth actually cultivates the power of sympathy, but the destruction of the other person's private self as a consequence of an imaginative engagement with him or her was not at all what Hawthorne's writings at Concord had envisaged: "then, at some inevitable moment, will the soul of the sufferer be dissolved, and flow forth in a dark, but transparent stream, bringing all its mysteries into the daylight."

Again, it is true that the "sympathies" of the crowd around the scaffold at the novel's conclusion are described by the narrator very positively. . . . But these people's response is both involuntary and at one level based on a misapprehension of the true state of affairs. This response is not properly conscious; neither does it embrace the full otherness of the man: "the people, whose great heart was thoroughly appalled, yet overflowing with tearful sympathy, as knowing that some deep life-matter—which, if full of sin, was full of anguish and repentances likewise—was now to be laid open to them." This is certainly not the deliberated, active workings of the sympathetic imagination as conceived in Hawthorne's earlier works. If the crowd had fully understood, it might well have condemned Dimmesdale ("[m]eagre, indeed, and cold, was the sympathy that a transgressor might look for, from such bystanders at the scaffold"), though it is possible that the deep emotion evoked by the tone of his voice rather than his words did prove stronger than socially instituted judgments, "beseeching its sympathy or forgiveness,—at every moment,—in each accent,—and never in vain!" This moment of understanding does not continue beyond his death, so what good it accomplishes unwittingly is profoundly limited. Moreover, it is notable that sympathy works here in this constructive way only when circumstances are rather impersonal (Hester the nurse, and the uncomprehending crowd around Dimmesdale) and when it does not have to deal with more disturbing feelings like hate, sexuality, or the sheer difference between individuals. . . .

Sympathy is presented as a necessary part of a child's development; it will also be shown to be essential to wider social interaction if these relationships are to escape the constricting framework of repressive ideologies. The word is used to explain Pearl's insulation from the social/symbolic order, when her mood of "perverse merriment" as she dances on tombstones removes her "entirely out of the sphere of sympathy or human contact.". . . When finally Pearl is fully inserted into the social order, this is achieved not simply through her father's public acknowledgment of her (which is socially misunderstood anyway): "The great scene of grief, in which the wild infant bore a part, had developed all her sympathies." "Sympathy" here is simply the capacity to sense what another may be feeling; it does not primarily mean pity, love, or caring, although the knowledge of others that sympathy brings does in this case lead to that.

In Hester's case, "sympathy" does stimulate the kind of benevolent action (Hester's care of the community's suffering) that the Salem tales had found important and that remains important. Such action is dependent on sympathy. Although charity takes second place in Hester's life to Dimmesdale and her daughter and may be construed as the transference of thwarted love, nonetheless "so much power to do, and power to sympathize" has considerable importance both in its immediate relief for sufferers, and more significantly in its success in effecting a major shift in the letter's social meaning and hence in Boston's symbolic order. We must grant, however, that the town also has other quite self-regarding reasons for liking Hester in this new but quite conventionally feminine role: "Able; so strong was Hester Prynne, with a woman's strength."

Nevertheless, although "sympathy" can then have benevolent effects with some people in certain circumstances, its essentially neutral nature allows it also to be an instrument to abuse others through the knowledge it brings. The sympathetic imagination had earlier in Hawthorne's work meant supportive recognition, revelation, and acceptance of those hidden parts of the subject unrepresented in the social order. *The Scarlet Letter* is deeply preoccupied with images of concealment, detection, exposure, revelation, truth, and being known to others, but it problematizes the notion of revelation and of truth to one's internal sense of being. Paradoxically the need to hide and protect part of oneself in the face of a threatening condemnatory world engenders an increasingly pressing desire within the consequently alienated being to be understood. . . .

This is the tightrope to be walked delicately between assuming a fallacious, hypocritical social mask and meeting the opprobrium consequent on total exposure. Hester's longing thoughts about explaining the letter to Pearl are again couched in terms of "sympathy"—connections and relationship, in this case a loving one ("The thought occurred to Hester, that the child might really be seeking to approach her with childlike confidence, and doing what she could, and as intelligently as she knew how, to establish a meeting-point of sympathy"). But dreading her antagonism, Hester lies to Pearl, and this lie ironically creates a greater gap between them: "'If this be the price of the child's sympathy, I cannot pay it!'" Dimmesdale is, one presumes, wholly sincere in his final attempt on the scaffold to confess (unlike his earlier two-faced efforts), but chance or hesitations of his rather less than directly expressed confession mean that loving pity is here evoked without the onlookers' having consciously to accommodate the "sinner" within their image of the saintly preacher.

SYMPATHY AND TRUTH ARE INSEPARABLE

Yet "sympathy" and "truth" are inextricably linked—"a glimpse of human affection and sympathy, a new life, and a true one" is how Dimmesdale conceives of it, though in his case the "sympathy" he then seeks is Boston's and the "truth" is Puritanically framed. This connection between personal integrity and a responsive social relationship is vital given the novel's basic conception of the human subject. Being "true" is dependent on being known, and this must involve mutual, benevolent acknowledgment—sympathy not just in the sense of the faculty that makes for knowledge, but sympathy in a morally positive responsive sense. This Chillingworth realizes, and having discovered Dimmesdale's secret, he deliberately and hence destructively withholds himself until Dimmesdale has a hysterically exaggerated notion of his corruption, concealment having become for the latter an even graver sin: "'Had I one friend,—or were it my worst enemy!—to whom, when sickened with the praises of all other men, I could daily betake myself, and be known as the vilest of all sinners, methinks my soul might keep itself alive thereby. Even thus much of truth would save me!'" Chillingworth, however, brings about his own self-destruction by a lack of truth to himself. In addition to hiding his feelings from others from the very first moment he enters Boston marketplace, he fails to acknowledge even to himself the strength of his own anger and frustration as he embarks on the search for his wife's lover, an emotional truth very different from the merely factual "truth" he thinks he is seeking.

The words "truth" and "true" pepper the text, sometimes centrally connected to the theme of revelation and that mirage of unified identity, sometimes merely as the narrator's attempt to establish some fact (for example, "it is true," "it may be true," "it might be true"), or as an exclamatory acknowledgment in dialogue ("'True!' replied he"). The overall effect is to jostle the reader repeatedly into an uneasy desire for certainty and the suspicion that this "truth" is not yet forthcoming. Dimmesdale's congregation is "hungry for the truth" of divine revelation; Chillingworth seeks his wife's lover, "'as I have sought truth in books; as I have sought gold in alchemy'"; and the reader, seeing both the illusory nature of the doctor's past pursuits and the ambiguities of "the judgment which Providence seemed about to work" in the final scene, is wary of trusting either books or God to deliver that "truth." The semantic variety of the word "truth" is itself testimony to the impossibility of unitary meaning.

Both Hester and Dimmesdale seem concerned with the "truth" of their feelings and actions, that is, they are concerned to establish some congruence, if not identity, between these two elements of their being (the mental life and existence in social relations). As we have seen, it is no longer a matter of "desire" opposing "circumstance," but matching consciousness and action within the social arena. "Truth" in this novel is used to cover a range of meanings with reference to a notion of psychic integrity, open relationships with others, and actions based on the adherence to some moral or metaphysical absolute. There is certainly no single truth: while Dimmesdale thinks there is a Christian one, Hester has evolved another based on an individual morality, and the narrator searches fairly unsuccessfully for some common base to both of these.

The primary meaning of "truth" is a psychological rather than an ethical one: the promise of "'Exchange this false life of shine for a true one'" is as much an observation of a psychological need as an assertion by Hester of the greater right of their love over conventional morality. When Dimmesdale meets Hester in the forest, their exchange has fullness, courage, and directness because, although they have different attitudes to their deed, there had been openness between them initially ("'We felt it so! We said so to each other!'"), and nothing can now remain concealed between them. This is so even if the social repercussions of this "truth" are nullified, and conventional morality would discern only a different kind of falsity: "Here, seen only by her eyes, Arthur Dimmesdale, false to God and man, might be, for one moment, true!" Chillingworth himself evinces a residual desire likewise to be known, exclaiming "'Dost thou know me so little, Hester Prynne?'" and later, breaking suddenly but momentarily from his obsession with torturing Dimmesdale to ponder with Hester (for there is no one else to talk to) over his miserable realization of his self-transformation: "'Dost thou remember me, Hester, as I was nine years agone?'"

In one respect Dimmesdale is correct in thinking that the letter aids Hester in "truth" in this sense—"'whom the scarlet letter has disciplined to truth, though it be the truth of red-hot iron, entering into the soul.'" But Dimmesdale's "life of ghastly emptiness" in "this dismal maze" is exacerbated by her need, until this point, to hide her husband from Dimmesdale: "'I must reveal the secret,' answered Hester firmly. 'He must discern thee in thy true character.'" Hester knows both the difficulty of telling the truth and the multiple repercussions for everyone, including Pearl, of failing to do so. Dimmesdale is also described in terms of a respect for "truth," when the complex psychology of truth-telling both underlies and undermines his far simpler notion about God's truth. By using the word "true" the narrator establishes how Dimmesdale has projected the complete fragmentation of the individual subject in psychological breakdown, emotional confusion, and loss of defined social role into images of divine condemnation, rejection, and annihilation: "that eternal alienation from the Good and True, of which madness is perhaps the earthly type.". . .

EACH MUST MAKE CHOICES

Choice is narrowed, then, partly because the needs and desires of other individuals must be faced, but partly too because this novel does not entertain for long the idea of a life beyond the frontiers of European culture. Subjectivity comes into being within a particular society, and so while Hester might posit that a short journey beyond the settlement will bring Dimmesdale to the place where he is "free"—the wilderness being the classic site for the independent Romantic subject in America—in practice existence is here conceived as inherently social, and there can be no such self-standing, let alone unified being beyond the settlement. Another way of looking at this is to say that Hester and Dimmesdale are themselves part of that social formation, and as such they influence its order and course in certain minor but unmistakable ways. Their subjectivity is not wholly contained by it, yet they help to constitute it. Hester may throw away the "fragments of a broken chain," but chains simultaneously link as well as bind, and so Pearl is raised on the edge of a community and taught its religious beliefs. . . .

Thus the novel comes to show that each person has a consciousness of having a "place" through personal and social relationships, whether or not these are officially sanctioned and generally recognized or not, and that, as the use of the word "home" shows, such positions within the social order may affirm self-definition in some way, however painful. For woman generally in this society, "home" has its traditional meaning of family dwelling and is conventionally her socially sanctioned arena: we can see how the word and image appears in Chillingworth's expectations and dreams of Hester, as well as in her hopes of a life together with Dimmesdale and their daughter. Hester, too, creates a home for Pearl in this primary sense, staving off Mistress Hibbins's subversive invitations with "'I must tarry at home, and keep watch over my little Pearl.'" Also conventionally, Dimmesdale can only find a "home" in the "midst of civilization and refinement," intending to flee to England, these New Englanders' intellectual and indeed childhood "home."

But the word shifts from these simple meanings when Hester decides to remain in Boston, scene of her adultery and shame and her lover's residence. Whereas her childhood home is "foreign" to her, she creates here in New England her "wild and dreary, but life-long home"—a phrase that seems paradoxical given the qualities conventionally assigned to "home," but that is subjectively meaningful. The rest of her life is similarly explained: she finally "found a home" in Boston, for here was the "home of so intense a former life." Mentally, her "home" is in the wilderness, but unless she accepts the compromises and partialities of life within the colony, she will have "home and comfort nowhere." Dimmesdale, ironically shepherded "home" at midnight by Chillingworth and again welcomed "home" by him after the forest meeting, is subjectively homeless until he mounts the scaffold.

"RESISTANCE AND ACCOMMODATION"

Thus situated within the social order, though only partially recognized or subliminally understood, these characters must content themselves with the presentation of "self" rather than full representation of themselves to society. The "Revelation of the Scarlet Letter" is an ironically entitled climax since not only does the town fail to understand but also the narrator refuses to describe the minister's stigmata even to the reader. Likewise, Hester is never fully revealed to the town. Given this perpetuation of ignorance and confusion, it is not surprising that Dimmesdale envisaged the Last Judgment as the chance "to see the dark problem of this life made plain," suggesting that "[a] knowledge of men's hearts will be needful to the completest solution of that problem." The obsession with a "talisman," an "open sesame," in Hawthorne's work now fades in the face of nonrevelation and conflicting claims. There are to be no comforting moral permanences here, only a counterpoint of resistance and accommodation, romantic love barely finding a niche there. Christian revelation, a possible transcendent solution to this "dark problem," may attract the narrator, but as far as the plot shows, it can provide only a happy death for Dimmesdale and not a promise to Hester. Divine revelation, if it comes, exists only in the afterlife. Hester's imagined "coming revelation"—a humanized and therefore more fragile version of truth-telling—also contains a Catch-22. It will depend on the teaching of a prophetess whose happy life will prove the truth of her vision of a new future society, yet it has already been made clear that present social structures will have to be torn down first before any woman can be happy. Hester remains therefore a prophetess without public power, her message only heard by the reader.

The Meaning of the Scarlet *A*

Claudia Durst Johnson

To be a literary classic, a book must continue to be meaningful to succeeding generations. Claudia Durst Johnson sets out to prove that *The Scarlet Letter* fulfills this test of time. She examines the complexity of the novel by first discussing the scarlet *A* as a symbol of adultery, then how it takes on additional meanings as the novel progresses. Johnson, professor of English at the University of Alabama and author of several articles and books on American literature, goes on to analyze various interpretations of the book, its four main characters, and the hidden human nature of the Puritan community.

What, in reality, is *The Scarlet Letter* "about"? It has all the ingredients of a soap opera, but it is far more than that. It could be a Puritan sermon, but it is surely not that, for the Puritans are not the heroes here. It is a story of passion, but the reader never sees what we would call an explicit sexual scene.

It is about the *consequences* of breaking the moral code, in this case a moral law. What happens to human beings as a result of such transgressions?

It is also about failing to be true to human nature. There are, in fact, many failings in this story: the failure of the Puritans; of the leaders; of the young wife, who thinks charitable actions coming from an uncharitable heart will make up for her moment of illicit passion; of the minister, her lover, who lies first to his community and then to himself; of the cold old man who seeks to ruin his young wife's lover.

It is a story about a terrible and cruel revenge worked out as the wronged old husband (who never reveals his true identity or his purpose) slowly injects his poison into the minds and the lives of all those around him.

From *Understanding* The Scarlet Letter: *A Student Casebook to Issues, Sources, and Historical Documents* by Claudia Durst Johnson. Copyright ©1995 by Claudia Durst Johnson. Reproduced with permission of Greenwood Publishing Group, Inc., Westport, Conn.

It is about the hypocrisy of members of a community who refuse to acknowledge that each of them is just as human, just as subject to passionate feelings as the woman they label an adulterer. If any novelist, any book can be said to have ripped the mask off Puritan pretensions, it is this writer, this book.

The Scarlet Letter is also about creativity—a person's attempt to see his or her own artistic side survive in a community that disapproves of the use of the imagination.

Furthermore, *The Scarlet Letter* is one of the earliest psychological novels in modern literature. It is one of the first works of fiction to probe the underside of human character—what lies unseen and unsaid beneath the surface. . . .

THE MEANINGS OF THE SCARLET LETTER

To get at the many meanings of the scarlet letter, it is useful to see, first, how it is represented in the child Pearl, who, the author tells us, is a little scarlet letter herself. Then the discussion will turn to the letter's meaning for the community, and finally, to its specific relationship to Hester, Dimmesdale, and Chillingworth.

While the letter has many *implied* meanings, it also has particular and explicit meanings. The first and most obvious is that Hester's "A" stands for adultery and, as the narrator puts it, "women's frailty and sinful passion." But the "A" on her breast begins to represent different things as Hester's story unfolds. For example, as a result of her charitable acts in the community, some people begin to think the "A" stands for able. And when the community sees a scarlet "A" in the sky on the night of John Winthrop's death, they believe it stands for angel. So, in the course of the novel, the "A" seems to encompass the entire range of human beingness, from the earthly and passionate "adulteress" to the pure and spiritual "angel," taking into account everything in between.

One begins to see many other human elements that the scarlet letter represents as the novel moves along. Pearl, for example, who is neither adulteress nor angel, is described as the living scarlet letter, and she embodies a full range of human characteristics: "Pearl's aspect was imbued with a spell of infinite variety; in this one child there were many children, comprehending the full scope between the wild-flower prettiness of a peasant baby, and the pomp, in little, of an infant princess." Furthermore, Hester begins to sense that many people besides herself wear scarlet letters on their breasts, even those with reputations for piety and purity:

> Could they be other than the insidious whispers of the bad angel, who would fain have persuaded the struggling woman, as yet only half his victim, that the outward guise of purity was but a lie, and that, if truth were everywhere to be shown, a scarlet letter would blaze forth on many a bosom besides Hester Prynne's? . . . Sometimes the red infamy upon her breast would give a sympathetic throb, as she passed near a venerable minister or magistrate, the model of piety and justice, to whom that age of antique reverence looked up as to a moral man in fellowship with angels. . . . Again, a mystic sisterhood would contumaciously assert itself as she met the sanctified frown of some matron, who, according to the rumor of all tongues, had kept cold snow within her bosom throughout life. That unsunned snow in the matron's bosom, and the burning shame on Hester Prynne's—what had the two in common? Or, once more, the electric thrill would give her warning—"Behold, Hester, here is a companion!"—and, looking up, she would detect the eyes of a young maiden glancing at the scarlet letter, shyly and aside, and quickly averted, with a faint, chill crimson in her cheeks as if her purity were somewhat sullied by that momentary glance.

The scarlet letter, in addition, has many implied meanings. "A" stands for Arthur Dimmesdale, for Hester's art, for Chillingworth's black or magical art. "A" can stand for atonement, which is what Hester is trying to do—atone for her sin with charitable acts. It also represents avenger or avenge, which is the whole purpose of Chillingworth's life. "A" represents the authority of the community that hypocritically condemns Hester for the rest of her life. It stands for Dimmesdale's ambition, as well as his anguish and agony. "A" represents the community, which is frequently characterized as aged or ancient.

PEARL

Much of the meaning of the scarlet letter resides in Pearl because she is the result of Hester's adultery. Hester dresses the child in scarlet, presenting her as a little scarlet letter. Moreover, Pearl has a morbid obsession with the scarlet letter. The connection is first made in the chapter entitled "The Governor's Hall," where her red dress is described. . . . Pearl's obsession with the letter her mother wears on her breast begins in infancy as her eyes focus on it. Then as a tiny girl, Pearl evinces a fascination with the letter and continually touches it and throws wild flowers at it. . . . Later, she begins to pester her mother with questions about why she wears the letter and what it means. In the forest scene when Hester takes off the scarlet letter, Pearl becomes frantically disturbed and won't quiet down until Hester has it back on her dress, as if by discarding the letter Hester has discarded Pearl. Pearl even makes herself an "A" from green seaweed. . . .

THE SCARLET *A*

Almost every critic who studies The Scarlet Letter *sees a different meaning for the scarlet A. In this excerpt from* Hawthorne's Tragic Vision, *author Roy R. Male lists his interpretations of this rich symbol.*

At the end we are left with the symbol into which the whole meaning of the book has been distilled. Around the letter have gathered not only the explicit associations of Adultress, Able, Affection, and Angel but also the myriad subtle suggestions of art, atonement, ascension, and the Acts of the Apostles. Here is the *A*, each limb of which suggests an ascension, with Pearl the link between the two; here is the sable background of the Puritan community; and fused in the entire symbol are the flesh and the spirit, the word and the light, the letter *A*, gules. Hawthorne seized upon the heraldic wording partly because of its rich poetic associations but also because "gules" is the perfect word with which to conclude the book. It means "scarlet," of course.

How does Pearl's connection with the scarlet letter bring us closer to its meanings? If she is identified with the scarlet letter, then the reader needs to consider her characteristics to determine some of the letter's meaning. First of all, Pearl is uncontrollable, subject to hyperactivity, bad temper, even behavior that could be classified as cruel. But for all her childish cruelty and hyperactivity, she is always depicted as nature's child. While the other children in the community play games taught by society and their parents, such as scourging Quakers and having prayer meetings, Pearl plays in the forest and by the seashore with living flora and fauna. The letter "A" she makes for herself is not red, but green— nature's color. These observations lead to the conclusion that the "A," rather than being exotic and lurid, as the community sees it, is in fact natural, and that those things associated with it—passion and sexuality in particular—are natural to human nature, not scarlet and demonic, as the community sees both the letter and Pearl herself. This would explain why Hester, metaphorically speaking, sees an "A" on many breasts other than her own: because passion exists as a natural part of human nature in every human being.

A second characteristic of Pearl shows that the scarlet letter means truth as well as nature. For all her faults, Pearl is the hardest truth-sayer in the novel. It is she who immediately recognizes Chillingworth as the "Black Man," or devil, in the community, telling Hester, "Come away, Mother! Come away, or yonder old Black Man will catch you! He hath got hold of the minister already." And it is she who suspects that Dimmesdale has a scarlet letter over his heart, asking Hester if she wears the scarlet letter for the same reason "that the minister keeps his hand over his heart!" She also knows intuitively that Hester is not telling her the truth about the letter. After Hester has lied about its meaning, Pearl will not let the matter drop. . . . Not only does she speak the truth, but she pursues the truth in continually questioning Hester about the meaning of the symbol she wears and the reason why Dimmesdale keeps his hand over his heart. From this connection of Pearl to truth, it is obvious that the scarlet letter, which Pearl embodies, is also a totality of truth about human nature and relationships. That at the end of the novel Pearl leaves America never to return suggests that those aspects of human nature on which the cold Puritans frown—in this case, creativity, passion, and joy—will not be acknowledged in New England for many years to come.

THE PURITAN COMMUNITY

The religious society of Boston, even though it is located in the New World, on the edge of uncharted wilderness, has little other affinity with nature and the natural; nor has the community acknowledged the full truth of the scarlet letter; nor is it tolerant of the whole range of human faculties, from angel to adulteress, that the letter represents. The people of the community, like their harsh ancestors whose portraits hang in the governor's mansion, gaze "with harsh and intolerant criticism at the pursuits and enjoyments of living men." Hester wears an "A" for her passion, but despite a theology that teaches that *all* people are innately, or by nature, evil, the community does not recognize that they themselves are sexual or passionate.

The narrator makes the reader aware of this secret, subtle intolerance early in the novel with stories of the Puritan community's suspicious intolerance of human nature, of those they see as different from themselves. This becomes dramatically clear in the harsh punishments imposed for trivial, natural human behavior.... The Puritan harshness of the community is reflected even in the play of the little children who imitate the actions of their elders. In marked contrast to Pearl, these children play at "scourging Quakers; or taking scalps in a sham-fight with the Indians; or scaring one another with freaks of imitative witchcraft."

Because they despise so many human traits, while at the same time failing to recognize those same passionate traits in themselves, Hester, always wearing the badge of adulterous love, becomes a target for their cruelty. It is almost as if the community can better deny the passion of their own nature by projecting it onto Hester and despising her for it. Even though, as we have seen, Hester perceptively senses the lust in the heart of even the most pious man of God and the purest maiden, the community acts as if she alone has passion in her heart....

HESTER

It is such a community that compels Hester Prynne to wear a scarlet letter as punishment for giving birth to an illegitimate child. In examining the meaning of the scarlet letter to Hester and her lover, Dimmesdale, it is important to note their relationship to both the letter "A" and to little Pearl, who so often represents the letter. It is appropriate that Hester, unlike the child's father, has to wear the badge of her passion for all to see, for by virtue of her biological nature, she cannot, as he can, hide the consequences of giving way to that desire. From the first, everyone sees that she is pregnant and that she gives birth to a child who then lives by her side, a reminder of what she is and has done always in full public view.

Hester gives the reader an important clue to her attitude when she immediately and richly embroiders the scarlet letter with gold thread. The community is outraged that she has made a mockery of her punishment by making this plain symbol of adultery into a gorgeous decoration.... If the "A," as we have seen, is a symbol of the full range of human nature, both of its base and its angelic qualities, then in assigning her an "A" of scarlet to wear as punishment, the community shows that it regards human nature, especially passion, to be devilish. And Hester, in embroidering the letter in gold, is trying to change her human reality, to make it prettier than it really is. She also is ashamed of her human nature. This can be seen in the way she dresses to present herself to the community, in somber gray hues and with her hair hidden under her cap. . . .

Even though she doesn't remove the scarlet letter publicly when Chillingworth tells her seven years later that the townspeople say she may, she does take it off privately in the forest. This action and Pearl's violent reaction to the removal of the letter seem to suggest that, even after seven years, she has not accepted the truth of her passionate nature (which is, of course, the truth of every person's nature, not just hers).

Hester's scarlet letter represents not only her creativity as a mother but her creativity as a seamstress. "A" also stands for her artistic nature. As the narrator writes of her sewing, "It was the art,—then, as now, almost the only one within a woman's grasp—of needlework." Yet, tutored as she is by her Puritan contemporaries, she also feels guilty about her art, and, in fact, about anything that gives her pleasure, as her art does: "Like all other joys, she rejected it as a sin."

So, as the narrator tells us, "the scarlet letter had not done its office." The community had intended that wearing it would cause Hester to feel repentant. But she doesn't. Rather than coming to believe that she must accept her true nature and love others in order to repent (in other words, that repentance must come from within), she believes that change should come from society, not within herself.

Hester's greatest self-deception, however, is believing that through her charitable acts within the community she can change her human nature and make up for what she is and has done. She has become a sister of mercy, ministering to the sick and dying, but she has no charity in her heart. To Dimmesdale in the forest she says, "Is there no reality in the penitence thus sealed and witnessed by good works?" In the same scene, the narrator concludes that the trials that Hester has endured because of the scarlet letter have "taught her much amiss."

Yet, ironically, it is what the scarlet letter represents that saves her: her pride, her passionate love for Dimmesdale, the child that she has created and embraced, and her vocation as an artist. . . .

DIMMESDALE

"A" also stands for Arthur; whether actually or metaphorically, Dimmesdale also wears a scarlet letter over his heart and is constantly aware of it. He knows that it is there, but he refuses to acknowledge it to the rest of the community, and rather than accepting the truth of his nature, he is tortured by it and tries to change it. This refusal is consistent with his rejection of Hester as his lover and Pearl as his child. But passion is nevertheless a decided part of Dimmesdale's basic nature. Indeed, "passion" is a word frequently used in describing what in most respects is a pale, passive man. . . .

Despite the fact that, like everyone else, he secretly wears a scarlet letter, he pretends to be saintly and self-sacrificing and full of Christian charity. He gives the community no hint that he is human, but fosters instead another, saintly role. He leads the community to think that he is too pure ever to consider a sexual union even in the bonds of matrimony: "he rejected all suggestions of the kind, as if priestly celibacy were one of his articles of church discipline." The congregation considers him to be a man of "especial sanctity.". . .

Not only is he guilty of self-deception, but Dimmesdale harbors other darker aspects of human nature as represented by the scarlet "A" in his heart. Above all, he conceals an "A" for ambition to which he will sacrifice anything. In following his overweening desire to be a great and revered minister in the Puritan world, he is selfish and egocentric—the very opposite of love. From first to last, Dimmesdale is most concerned not with his own soul, not with Hester's pain, but with what other people think about him and how it will affect his career. When Pearl asks him to stand on the scaffold with them in the daylight, he panics; "all the dread of public exposure that had so long been the anguish of his life had returned upon him.". . .

But still Dimmesdale's hidden scarlet letter represents more than passion, adultery, and concern for self. It also stands for artist and author, which words describe his profession as a writer of sermons. For just as Hester creates art with her needle and thread, Dimmesdale creates art with the words he delivers from the pulpit. His art is described as almost magical, hypnotic, reaching his parishioners "in gushes of sad, persuasive eloquence." For this ambition in his vocation as an artful minister, he sacrifices his child and lover and the truth of his heart. One might even argue that for ambition he sacrifices love.

Dimmesdale's "A" at last represents "anguish" and "agony," words frequently used in describing him. He acknowledges these qualities to himself, believing that his own pain and suffering are in fact far greater than Hester's. Still, the question arises as to whether this also is a self-delusion, especially when the reader realizes that Hester's agony and anguish have caused her to contemplate murdering Pearl and committing suicide: "At times, a fearful doubt strove to possess her soul, whether it were not better to send Pearl at once to heaven, and go herself to such futurity as Eternal Justice should provide." Yet despite all that, Dimmesdale's agony is still not enough to drive him to reveal the truth about himself.

CHILLINGWORTH

Chillingworth, in his connection with the scarlet letter, is the worst of the Puritan community. He is always identified as the devil or the devil's emissary, as an "archfiend." Pearl, who sees through everyone, is the first to associate him with Satan. And by the time of Hester's last private interview with him, just before she reveals his identity to Dimmesdale, she also sees him as a satanic figure in the form of a bat.

He is the epitome of cold intellect and old age, without the full range of redeeming qualities generated by the heart and soul. He has been a scholar in Europe and passes for a medical scholar in the New World. In Hester's memory of him, even when they married, he was already old and wedded to his books. She remembers him as "a man well stricken in years, a pale, thin, scholar-like visage, with eyes dim and bleared by the lamplight that had served them to pore over many ponderous books." In the jail after Hester has stood on the scaffold, Chillingworth describes himself as "a man of thought, the bookworm of great libraries—a man already in decay, having given my best years to feed the hungry dream of knowledge.". . .

Chillingworth's evil character—like something right out of melodrama—is also reflected in his physical appearance. As his human faculties become more and more out of balance—his intellect becoming overdeveloped at the expense of his heart—one side of his body becomes out of balance with the other. Even when he married Hester, this man of the study and laboratory already had a humped back. His deformity of body finally represents a deformity of character in which heart and soul play little part. As a result, he becomes at last bent over toward the ground, more like a snake than a human being. . . .

Chillingworth's "A" may also stand for alchemist and artist, for he is both. While intent on probing into Dimmesdale's heart, he says that he is determined to continue, "were it only for the art's sake." Later he tells Hester, "What art can do, I have exhausted on him." Unlike Hester's creative art, however, his is a wholly destructive black art, clearly meaning black magic and witchcraft. Some in the community are suspicious of his connection with Dr. Forman, a man accused of witchcraft in England, and also suspect that among the Indians he may have picked up what is described as "their skill in the black art." This refers to the Puritans' early beliefs that God had prepared a way for them in the wilderness and that the native Indians were minions of the devil.

CONCLUSION

The close association of Chillingworth (who, as avenger, becomes the Black Man or devil) with the community creates a number of ironies. These affinities are established as soon as Chillingworth enters the community, when they rejoice that he, the old physician, can treat the ailing young minister Dimmesdale, who initially, and secretly, rejects this. Despite Dimmesdale's resistance, however, the community successfully elevates Chillingworth and presses Dimmesdale to move in with the "leech": "There was much joy throughout the town when this greatly desirable object was attained." By this time, however, some of the community sense something unsavory about Chillingworth, one of them reporting that Chillingworth had been connected with "Doctor Forman, the famous old conjurer." But the community leaders, of course, are the ones who prevail.

From this allegiance of Chillingworth and the community come several other ironies. While the community thinks that the Black Man abides in the forest, he actually abides among them in the form of their honored guest and "healer," Chillingworth. And while the community believes that witchcraft is practiced somewhere in the depths of the forest, the most heinous black magic is practiced with their approval and cooperation right under their noses in Chillingworth's laboratory.

The conclusion that the reader is given to draw, then, is that Hester and Pearl are not respectively, lover and daughter of a Black Man or Satan who inhabits the forest. Rather it is the community itself which has a close relationship to the Black Man, in the person of Chillingworth, and encourages his dark arts.

Finally, in exploring the meaning of the "A," the reader arrives at Hawthorne's stated moral: "Be true! Be true! Be true! Show freely to the world, if not your worst, yet some trait whereby the worst may be inferred!" The true nature of every human is both sinful and angelic, somber and joyful, selfish and loving. To "be true" means to recognize that we all wear a scarlet letter.

The Relevance of "The Custom House"

John E. Becker

Literary critics have been debating the merits of
The Scarlet Letter's introductory essay, "The Custom
House," since it was first published in 1850. Some
say it is not related to *The Scarlet Letter*; others claim
that its mention of a scarlet *A* is a direct introduction
to the novel. John E. Becker, Hawthorne scholar and
literary critic, discusses the structure of "The Custom House," especially its division into four phases,
arguing that it is essential to the work.

The fact that the story of *The Scarlet Letter* seems to have no
intrinsic dependence on its introductory essay has caused
many critics to reject it, among them, W.C. Brownell, Austin
Warren, and Edward Wagenknecht. But there is an increasing body of criticism which finds that "The Custom-House"
adds important dimensions to the whole. Charles Feidelson,
in *Symbolism and American Literature,* binds the two parts
of the fictional structure together with an epistemological
theme: how a symbol acquires meaning. In "The Custom-
House" we see Hawthorne absorbed in the contemplation of
the letter. In the story proper each character re-enacts Hawthorne's contemplation in his own way and with his own results. It seems necessary, however, to add to this epistemological concern a moral and psychological concern which is
more central to the experience of the novel. . . .

Other critics who have addressed themselves to the problem of the unity of preface and story have brought out parallels between Hawthorne and Dimmesdale and Hawthorne
and Hester, as well as contrasts between Hawthorne's Custom-House milieu and Puritan times. The present analysis is
an attempt to show how all of these insights into the unity of
Hawthorne's work are rooted in the literary form of allegory

From *Hawthorne's Historical Allegory: An Examination of the American Conscience* by
John E. Becker (Port Washington, NY: Kennikat Press, 1971). Copyright ©1971 by John
E. Becker. Reprinted by permission of the author.

as Hawthorne recreated it. To return to the allegorical tradition, what do we see when we regard "The Custom-House" as a prefatory statement-of-intention like the traditional prefaces to the allegories of [Edmund] Spenser and [John] Bunyan?

TRADITIONAL PREFACES

Hawthorne himself throws us off the track by disclaiming any structural function for "The Custom-House." He refers to his earlier "autobiographical impulse," the one which inspired "The Old Manse," as inexcusable. He had given in to that impulse "for no earthly reason, that either the indulgent reader or the intrusive author could imagine." The only reason "The Custom-House" is being written, then, is that "beyond my deserts, I was happy enough to find a listener or two on the former occasion." In other words, this essay is as irrelevant to the fiction of *The Scarlet Letter* as that one was to the looser structure of *Mosses from an Old Manse.* But Hawthorne's modest authorial disclaimers and surface apologies are not to be trusted any more than his claim to be merely the editor of the story of *The Scarlet Letter.* The relationships among writer, reader, and work had changed since the times of Spenser and Bunyan. The element of irony in Hawthorne's prefaces is not merely an expression of his own ironic and skeptical personality. It is, as we shall see, a result of the change in the fictional situation. We must do the best we can to infer Hawthorne's intentions, since we cannot expect him to state them. Not only "The Custom-House" but the earlier essay, "The Old Manse," to which Hawthorne alludes as a parallel instance of "the autobiographical impulse," give us the little evidence we have about what Hawthorne wanted to do in writing *The Scarlet Letter.* . . .

Hawthorne, then, does not write a traditional preface to a traditional allegory to tell us what he intends to do. Rather, in the course of the two prefatory essays, "The Old Manse" and "The Custom-House" he asks all the questions an author can ask of himself about the significance of his writing. His answers do not orchestrate a resounding affirmation of the importance of his work. He leaves us to judge that for ourselves. All he will say is that he is laying himself on the line, and doing so with a full awareness of his own serious commitment. He will say something significant, in spite of all that may be adduced by himself or by others against that possibility.

THE FOUR PHASES

Hawthorne develops the Custom-House essay in four phases which, though they interpenetrate, remain more or less distinct. He presents himself to the reader; he describes his daily life in the Custom-House; he "discovers" the scarlet letter; finally, he is liberated to write his novel. An examination of the functions served by each of these phases of "The Custom-House" will make it possible to propose a hypothesis not only for unifying the essay itself, but also for integrating it into the overall fictional structure which Hawthorne produced.

At the beginning of "The Custom-House" Hawthorne invites us, as surely as any Walt Whitman, to commune with his soul. Hawthorne was a romantic, and he would like us to be among "the few who will understand him, better than most of his schoolmates and lifemates." But the strong defensive tone makes the mention of Whitman seem incongruous. Hawthorne is decidedly not like "some authors" who:

> indulge themselves in such confidential depths of revelation as could fittingly be addressed, only and exclusively, to the one heart and mind of perfect sympathy; as if the printed book, thrown at large on the wide world, were certain to find out the divided segment of the writer's own nature, and complete his circle of existence by bringing him into communion with it.

Hawthorne is concerned to keep "the inmost Me behind its veil," and to do this he allows us the strictly defined role of "friend, a kind and apprehensive, though not the closest friend." With this understanding of the relationship between writer and reader clarified, Hawthorne proceeds through the Custom-House setting and an explanation of his ancestral ties to Salem, to present himself with clear dimensions in space and time.

Hawthorne wants us to meet him precisely in the setting of the Custom-House and at that time of his career. His description of the Custom-House is detailed, exact, vivid as the writing of his American Notebooks had taught him to be. But he is not simply giving "a faint representation of a mode of life not heretofore described." His thematic concerns are at work as well. He evokes the dull atmosphere of the place and the lazy unresponsiveness of the people by contrasting them with a time when the busy world of commerce had not yet passed Salem by. The slovenly emptiness of his office is described with the same detail, and it is here that he arranges for our introduction:

> And here, some six months ago,—pacing from corner to corner, or lounging on the long-legged stool, with his elbow on the desk, and his eyes wandering up and down the columns of the morning newspaper,—you might have recognized, honored reader, the same individual who welcomed you into his cheery little study, where the sunshine glimmered so pleasantly through the willow branches, on the western side of the Old Manse.

The obvious incongruity of the man and the setting, reinforced by the allusion to the very different setting of the Old Manse, must strike the reader as a suggestion in advance of the kind of incongruities which will be developed in *The Scarlet Letter.* As the world of the Custom-House was totally unwilling and unable to take account of the rich sensibilities of an artist like Hawthorne, so the world of the Puritans was unwilling and unable to take account of the rich femininity of a woman like Hester. Hawthorne was stifled by this indifferent world, and it is not at all surprising that his experience of that world should project itself as a major theme of the story which evolves out of his Custom-House experience. . . .

HAWTHORNE'S TIES WITH SALEM

Another thematic parallel between the essay and the novel is Hawthorne's discussion of his ancestral ties with Salem. There is a certain fatality, attributable to Hawthorne's ambivalent but strong feelings about his ancestors, which explains his return to Salem and his assumption of the post of surveyor. Those ancestors were a present reality to him. They bound him, at least for the moment, to the place, as Hester's ties to her Puritan world bound her to stay and live out her punishment. Hawthorne too is living out a kind of punishment—a punishment incurred by the severity of his first ancestor toward a woman not altogether unlike the heroine of Hawthorne's story:

> He was likewise a bitter persecutor; as witness the Quakers, who have remembered him in their histories, and relate an incident of his hard severity towards a woman of their sect, which will last longer, it is to be feared, than any record of his better deeds, although these were many.

Hawthorne is able to pay off the debt incurred by this ancestor because he is so fully endowed with a sensibility which understands and shares the plight of a woman like Hester.

The care with which Hawthorne builds up the setting in

which he introduces himself to his reader has a function, however, that goes beyond the mere suggestion of themes that will be important in the novel. This function is structural, an element of the fictional form. If we return once more to that carefully guarded distance established between the author and his reader, we may further reflect that the distance that Hawthorne has established is not simply a distance between author and reader, but a distance between reader and story as well. Here, I think, is the central purpose of Hawthorne's introduction of himself in "The Custom-House."

The aim, in a realistic novel, is to make the reader feel that the story world is not a story world at all, but a simple presentation of reality as it is. One aspect of this is that the creator hides himself from the reader. The absence of the authorial personality sets up an unspoken understanding between creator and reader that there is an identity between their points of view. By the artistry of the writer, the reader is induced to immerse himself in the story world, in its places and events, in its values, too, because the reader has been made to feel that the story world is simply his own world, and not the product of another human imagination. Of course, the reader who comes to a realistic novel with his critical faculties fully alert may not allow himself to enter so fully into the world of the novel, but it is not impossible that this kind of sophistication may in some cases be a block to the specific kind of artistic experience which is particular to the realistic novel. . . .

To place oneself, however, as Hawthorne does, clearly and boldly before the reader is to create a different kind of relationship between the reader and the story than the one established by the techniques of realism or by traditional narrative in general. Because the author's presence is explicit, the story world he presents exists precisely as *his* world, created, fabricated by him. It is an "other world," not the reader's own world, and so he neither immerses himself in it, nor discovers himself immersed in it, but regards it from the outside, contemplatively. The story is kept at a sufficient emotional distance for us to stand apart and look for its meaning.

This difference in the mode of existence of a story world whose creator is present relates to what we have observed about the allegorical world of some of the sketches. Within the framework of authorial presence created by the historical essay the actual story evokes an almost surrealistic world, in which events proceed in ritual progression and are interconnected by an implicit magical causality. We recognize this world as Hawthorne's world of "romance," but we also see the effect as more than merely atmospheric.... The author, by insisting upon his own presence, keeps us outside the story world he creates, in order to keep our interpretative faculties alert for the more explicitly intellectual task he has put before us.

The effect is maintained throughout "The Custom-House" by the continued autobiographical tone, but it is also continued in the novel proper. Hawthorne interjects into the narrative of *The Scarlet Letter* a steady punctuation of brief historical essays addressed directly to the reader. They keep the story anchored in its historical setting, and they keep the author clearly in view.

Primarily, then, Hawthorne's introduction of himself at the beginning of "The Custom-House" orients the reader toward a more detached and intellectualized fictional world. Secondarily, certain central themes of the novel find their parallels in the sensibilities of Hawthorne himself: the contrast between the sensitive individual and the obtuse world of ordinary men, the ambivalent emotional bonds of love, hate, and guilt which bind people to the place of their deepest suffering.

THE SECOND PHASE

The second phase of the Custom-House essay consists of two somewhat extended character sketches set among Hawthorne's witty reflections on the people who populated the Custom-House and their influence on his ability to create literature. Here the theme of incongruity between the author and his associates becomes more important. Hawthorne maintains the proportion: Hawthorne is to the Custom-House world as Hester is to the Puritan world, but he takes it a step farther. Just as Hester is able to turn the tables on her punishers by making the scarlet letter signify angel rather than adulteress without herself repenting; so Hawthorne, by his seemingly harmless and irrelevant skill as a writer is able to make the impervious world of Custom-House veterans wince with pain. Hawthorne's smooth syntax proves to be the gleam on a destructive weapon which Hawthorne enjoyed and used freely. And he felt quite justified, in his own sardonic way:

> It is a pious consolation to me, that, through my interference, a sufficient space was allowed them for repentance of the evil and corrupt practices, into which, as a matter of course, every Custom-House officer must be supposed to fall. Neither the front nor the back entrance of the Custom-House opens on the road to Paradise.

Hawthorne's most destructive blow is the character sketch of the "permanent Inspector." With a cheerfulness and good nature that never suggests invective, Hawthorne empties this man of all human qualities, leaving him a kind of harmless beast. His sketch is the more damaging because he follows it with the more extended and truly admiring sketch of the "old General." The two figures are at opposite ends of the scale of humanity.

One of the most interesting points of comparison between the two men, in the light of the themes of "The Custom-House," is the different ways they live in relation with their past. . . .

LINKS WITH THE PAST

Hawthorne creates two still-living links with the Puritan past, each of whom manifests qualities of that past which are important in the story of Hester Prynne. One represents the final reduction to animality of Puritan materialism and insensitivity to human feeling. The other represents the dying fire of the nobility and idealism which was the inspiring motive behind the whole Puritan enterprise. What Hawthorne sees around him, in this dull and moribund world of Custom-House veterans is the crumbled remains of a world which was once able to hold these qualities in tension so that moral issues, at least for some, were as deeply serious as they are for him.

Hawthorne is proud of the flexibility in his nature which allowed him to associate with the members of such a totally foreign milieu. It is a point of pride with him that the overwhelming dullness and decay of that world did not win out against him, but rather enlivened his sense of irony. Eventually he made the indifferent Custom-House world wince at the power of his pen. There is, then, a kind of ultimate irony which inspires Hawthorne to place the discovery of *The Scarlet Letter* within this backwater of decay and death. Hawthorne's consistent technique of anchoring his stories of the American past in the American present gains a certain piquancy here. Within a society of decaying human spirits amid its piles of useless bureaucratic scribbling, Hawthorne comes upon a symbol which will carry him back into the intense vitality of its past.

THE SCARLET *A*

Hawthorne constructs the fictitious narration of his discovery of the letter to arouse suspense. He moves from an idle curiosity appropriate to the oppressive dullness of the Custom-House to an almost obsessive contemplation of the letter and an imperious feeling of filial duty to tell the story. And as this transformation within Hawthorne himself is dramatized, he prods the curiosity of the reader by a kind of forward-backward movement from vagueness to clarity. The steps of discovery are rapid enough, but Hawthorne persistently diverts interest into details that delay the movement of the narration. We are first diverted by Mr. Pue, his commission, and what was left of him when his body was exhumed. What we first find is only a scrap of faded red cloth with a certain mysterious quality from its being the work of a lost art. When we finally perceive that it is the letter *A* we are again side-tracked by Hawthorne into thinking of it as a badge of honor. We are left with a final mystery-making puzzle—the burning sensation which Hawthorne felt in his breast when he placed the letter there.

What Hawthorne has elicited here is a clear demand for interpretation of the letter. And this demand for interpretation which he himself has placed in the reader is his way of alerting us to the fact that in reading *The Scarlet Letter* we are reading an allegory. . . . For Hawthorne, the dream technique is usually more subtly employed. It is less an initial clue to allegory than it is a pervasive quality of the whole work. Hawthorne prefers to confront the reader, as he does here, with a physical object that demands interpretation. As he tells the story of the discovery of the letter, he himself plays with its possible meanings and induces us to do so by the sense he gives of freedom to indulge in such a play of the mind. There is no predetermined meaning. We contemplate it with him. And this is Hawthorne's clearest and most explicit invitation to allegory.

Hawthorne does not present us, then, with an invitation to solve an allegorical puzzle to which he himself knows the solution because he constructed it. There is more than an intellectual puzzle here. There is, he suggests, a connection so deep and so intimate between himself and what the letter represents that the touch of the symbol creates a burning sensation, causes an involuntary shudder, involves him and us in a process which is deeply personal, for all its contemplative detachment. Hawthorne's own experience of the scarlet *A* in "The Custom-House" is an integral part of the allegorical structure which he creates, as he will remind us at the end of the novel when he tells us how oppressive has been his concern with it. Hawthorne's experience of the letter *is* the allegory which we read in reading *The Scarlet Letter.*

If this is the case, Hawthorne must make explicit the relationship between himself and the past from which the letter came. He does not simply set his story in the past, he establishes himself in his own present and then moves by explicit and precisely measured steps into the particular moment of the letter. When we learn of surveyor Pue we are told that he died an exact eighty years ago. And we are given an even more vivid sense of his antiquity when we are presented with the picture of his exhumed skeleton and its well-preserved wig. We are made to feel the movement back, to experience the pastness. Then, by a second clearly distinct step we move from the times of Pue back to the figure of Hester herself through the medium of the oral testimony of the old people of the time of Pue. Oral testimony is here, as always, tinged with the quality of myth. Hawthorne achieves, by these measured steps into the past, more than just the desired aura of romance, the heightening of shadows and the clarity of outline which comes from a distant perspective in time. He emphasizes that the movement back in time is a part of the meaning of his story, a part of the structure of his fiction. Again, it is Hawthorne's own experience of the parallels and the contrasts between that distant time and his own present world which constitutes the allegory. This is to say again what has been said before, that Hawthorne is the hero of *The Scarlet Letter.* . . .

THE FINAL PHASE

The final phase of "The Custom-House" describes Hawthorne's futile efforts to create his story while still employed in the Custom-House and the creative release which came with the loss of his position. In the course of describing his difficulties he gives us a detailed account of the famed aura of romance which he tried to create in his fiction. His romantic world had to be a neutral area between the real and the imaginary, suffused by a cold light which spiritualizes (the moon), and a warm light which gives humanity (the coal fire). This world must exist ideally, like a mirror image, at one remove from reality. Though he is tempted away from this, his preferred fictional world, by the siren call of realism, he recognizes that it is not in him to be able to penetrate to the deeper import of the every-day world. It is his own interior war with the contemporary world which causes Hawthorne's melancholy. It frightens him with the possibility that he will become another animal-like old man, his mind able to focus no further than the next meal. What he sees slipping from his grasp is precisely the faculty which distinguishes him from these old men—the power to live free of the contemporary world, to live throughout the whole range of his sensibility, to seek out his adventures among the world of unrealities. Once he is liberated from the Custom-House and sets out to write his story, happiness returns: "he was happier, while straying through the gloom of these sunless fantasies, than at any time since he had quitted the Old Manse."

Chronology

1803

U.S. buys Louisiana from France.

1804

Nathaniel Hawthorne is born July 4 at Salem, Massashusetts.

1804–1806

Lewis and Clark explore American Northwest.

1812–1815

War with Great Britain.

1813

Injures his foot and is kept out of school for two years.

1819

America acquires Florida from Spain.

1825

Graduates from Bowdoin College; Erie Canal opens.

1828

Self-publishes his first novel, *Fanshawe;* Baltimore and Ohio Railroad establishes first passenger railroad in U.S.; Andrew Jackson elected president.

1830

Publishes anonymously his first stories in the Salem *Gazette* and in the *Token*, an annual Boston publication.

1833

American Anti-Slavery Society formed.

1837

Publishes *Twice-Told Tales;* meets Sophia Peabody.

1838

Hawthorne and Sophia become engaged.

1839

First political appointment, measurer at the Boston Custom-House, brings him a salary of fifteen hundred dollars a year.

1841

Overland migration to California starts; in April joins the Utopian community at Brook Farm, but leaves in November.

1842

Hawthorne and Sophia marry and settle into the Old Manse in Concord, Massachusetts; publishes an enlarged edition of *Twice-Told Tales*.

1846

Friends in the Democratic Party arrange for Hawthorne's appointment as surveyor at the Salem Custom-House; publishes *Mosses from an Old Manse*.

1848

Gold discovered in California; gold rush starts.

1849

Loses surveyor post in new Whig administration; begins his most productive period of writing.

1850

Publishes *The Scarlet Letter*.

1851

New York Times established; publishes *The House of the Seven Gables*, a romance that, like *The Scarlet Letter*, studies the effects of an unpardonable sin.

1852

Publishes *The Blithedale Romance* and writes campaign biography of Franklin Pierce; also publishes *A Wonder-Book for Girls and Boys*, a retelling of some classical myths.

1853

After publishing *Tanglewood Tales*, a sequel to *Wonder-Book*, appointed by President Pierce to the post of consul at Liverpool, England.

1854

Republican party formed.

1855

Walt Whitman publishes *Leaves of Grass*.

1857

Resigns consulship; he and Sophia spend two months in England before going to Italy for an extended stay; Supreme Court makes Dred Scott decision.

1860

Publishes *The Marble Faun*, a novel set in Rome; returns with Sophia to Wayside.

1863

Publishes *Our Old Home*, a volume of sketches of travels and life in England.

1864

On a trip with Pierce intended to improve his health, Hawthorne dies in Plymouth, New Hampshire; buried in Sleepy Hollow Cemetery in Concord; Lincoln reelected president.

1865

Lee surrenders at Appomattox; Lincoln assassinated.

FOR FURTHER RESEARCH

ABOUT HAWTHORNE'S LIFE AND TIMES

Newton Arvin, *Hawthorne*. Boston: Little, Brown, 1929.

Sculley Bradley, Richmond Croom Beatty, E. Hudson Long, and Seymour Gross, eds., *Nathaniel Hawthorne: The Scarlet Letter: An Authoritative Text, Backgrounds and Sources, Criticism*. 2nd ed. New York: W.W. Norton, 1978.

Julian Hawthorne, *Nathaniel Hawthorne and His Wife*. Boston: James R. Osgood, 1885.

Hubert H. Hoeltje, *Inward Sky: The Mind and Heart of Nathaniel Hawthorne*. Durham, NC: Duke University Press, 1962.

David Laskin, *A Common Life: Four Generations of American Literary Friendship and Influence*. New York: Simon and Schuster, 1994.

James R. Mellow, *Nathaniel Hawthorne in His Times*. Boston: Houghton Mifflin, 1979.

Edwin Haviland Miller, *Salem Is My Dwelling Place: A Life of Nathaniel Hawthorne*. Iowa City: University of Iowa Press, 1991.

Lloyd Morris, *The Rebellious Puritan: Portrait of Mr. Hawthorne*. New York: Harcourt, Brace, 1927.

Randall Stewart, *Nathaniel Hawthorne: A Biography*. New Haven, CT: Yale University Press, 1948.

Arlin Turner, *Nathaniel Hawthorne: A Biography*. New York: Oxford University Press, 1980.

ABOUT *THE SCARLET LETTER*

Nina Baym, *The Shape of Hawthorne's Career*. Ithaca, NY: Cornell University Press, 1976.

John E. Becker, *Hawthorne's Historical Allegory: An Examination of the American Conscience.* Port Washington, NY: Kennikat Press, 1971.

Michael Davitt Bell, *Hawthorne and the Historical Romance in New England.* Princeton, NJ: Princeton University Press, 1971.

Millicent Bell, *Hawthorne's View of the Artist.* Albany: State University of New York Press, 1962.

Richard H. Brodhead, *Hawthorne, Melville, and the Novel.* Chicago: University of Chicago Press, 1973.

Michael Colacurcio, ed., *New Essays on* The Scarlet Letter. Cambridge, England: Cambridge University Press, 1985.

Frederick Crews, *The Sins of the Fathers: Hawthorne's Psychological Themes.* Berkeley: University of California Press, 1966.

J. Donald Crowley, *Hawthorne: The Critical Heritage.* New York: Barnes and Noble, 1970.

Edward H. Davidson, *Hawthorne's Last Phase.* New Haven, CT: Yale University Press, 1966.

Alison Easton, *The Making of the Hawthorne Subject.* Columbia: University of Missouri Press, 1996.

Kenneth Marc Harris, *Hypocrisy and Self-Deception in Hawthorne's Fiction.* Charlottesville: University Press of Virginia, 1988.

Claudia Durst Johnson, *Understanding* The Scarlet Letter*: A Student Casebook to Issues, Sources, and Historical Documents.* Westport, CT: Greenwood Press, 1995.

A.N. Kaul, ed., *Hawthorne: A Collection of Critical Essays.* Englewood Cliffs, NJ: Prentice-Hall, 1966.

A. Robert Lee, ed., *Nathaniel Hawthorne: New Critical Essays.* Totowa, NJ: Barnes and Noble, 1982.

Roy R. Male, *Hawthorne's Tragic Vision.* New York: W.W. Norton, 1957.

Gary Scharnhorst, *The Critical Response to Nathaniel Hawthorne's* The Scarlet Letter. New York: Greenwood Press, 1992.

Leland Schubert, *Hawthorne the Artist: Fine-Art Devices in Fiction.* Chapel Hill: University of North Carolina Press, 1944.

Mark Van Doren, *Nathaniel Hawthorne: A Critical Biography*. New York: William Sloane, 1949.

Edward C. Wagenknecht, *Nathaniel Hawthorne: Man and Writer*. New York: Oxford University Press, 1961.

Hyatt H. Waggoner, *Hawthorne: A Critical Study*. Cambridge, MA: Harvard University Press, 1963.

ABOUT HAWTHORNE'S PLACE IN AMERICAN LITERATURE

Van Wyck Brooks, *The Flowering of New England: 1815–1865*. New York: Dutton, 1936.

Richard Chase, *The American Novel and Its Tradition*. Garden City, NY: Doubleday, 1957.

Scott Donaldson and Ann Massa, *American Literature: Nineteenth and Twentieth Centuries*. New York: Barnes and Noble, 1978.

Carl Van Doren, *The American Novel: 1789–1939*. Rev. and enl. ed. New York: Macmillan, 1940.

WORKS BY
NATHANIEL HAWTHORNE

Fanshawe (1828)

"The Hollow of Three Hills" published in the *Salem Gazette* (1830)

Twenty-two stories published in the *Token* (1831–1837)

Twice-Told Tales, first edition (1837)

Grandfather's Chair; Famous Old People; Liberty Tree (1841)

Twice-Told Tales, second edition; *Biographical Stories for Children* (1842)

Mosses from an Old Manse (1846)

The Scarlet Letter (1850)

The House of the Seven Gables; Twice-Told Tales, third edition; *The Snow Image and Other Twice-Told Tales; True Stories from History and Biography* (1851)

A Wonder-Book for Girls and Boys; Life of Pierce; The Blithedale Romance (1852)

Tanglewood Tales for Girls and Boys (1853)

Mosses from an Old Manse, revised edition (1854)

The Marble Faun (1860)

Our Old Home (1863)

POSTHUMOUS PUBLICATIONS

Passages from the American Notebooks (1868)

Passages from the English Notebooks (1870)

Passages from the French and Italian Notebooks (1871)

Septimius Felton (1872)

The Dolliver Romance (1876)

Dr. Grimshawe's Secret; The Ancestral Footstep (1883)

INDEX

8/05   16   12/04
10/ 9 (26)
5/16 (31) 8/15